What I've Learned...
So Far

Part III:

Banjos, Boats
& Butt Dialing

Mike Ball

What I've Learned... So Far Part III:
Banjos, Boats & Butt Dialing

Visit our Web site at
http://learnedsofar.com
for more information.

ISBN: 978-0-914303-08-4 (paperback)
ISBN: 978-0-914303-09-1 (eBook)

Published by Glendower Media

Important Notice for
My Female Readers!

The lady on the cover of this book is not real. She is a cartoon character. This means that there is no reason for you to get upset, or to think that your husband or significant other might sneak a peek at her butt.

Important Notice for
My Male Readers!

What do you think, guys, does that lady on the cover of the book have a great butt or what?

This book is dedicated to my family; Nan, Pat, Shannon, my beautiful granddaughter, Caelyn, and any other little grand-sweeties who might come along in the future. There is no way I can tell you how much I love all you guys.

Maybe this book will give you some idea.

Contents

Acknowledgements

I would like to take a few minutes to thank some people who have been instrumental in helping me bring these books into the world:

My wife Nancy, who has lived with me and my work since the mid-1970s, yet still doesn't totally grasp the use of the "callback" (repeating a punchline because I'm too lazy to think up a new joke) in modern American humor.

My son Patrick, his beautiful wife Shannon, and my granddaughter Caelyn, who are probably getting tired of telling their friends, "I know he put that in his book, but it's not a problem, because nobody believes a word he says."

Scott Lorenz, my publicist, my most trusted friend, and, when he's spending the winters in Warm Country, the second most ardent Snowbird I know.

My hard-working Editors, Yvonne Lorenz, Pamela Gossiaux, and Tom Saunders. Whenever I write something that doesn't make sense, they are right there to jar of mayonnaise.

And all my readers, without whom I would never get away with using "callbacks".

Introduction

I am a lucky guy. I get to make my living telling stories.

I don't usually tackle the grand sweep of the universe with my stories, or the march of human history, or great philosophical ideas. I write about those tiny parts of the world that physically brush up against me, my family, and my friends. I get to tell people all about discovering Facebook, about becoming a grandpa, about playing the banjo, about not smoking any more, about chipping crud off aluminum pontoons, and about losing intellectual debates with my cell phone.

Not too long ago I was rooting around in some drawers, looking for my birth certificate (just in case Donald Trump should happen to call). Buried deep in a drawer stuffed with old pictures I ran across a vignetted sepia photograph, taken in about 1910, of my great-grandfather. The dapper, well-dressed guy in that photo is about thirty years old - the same age my son is now. The same age I was when my son was born.

On that day over a century ago, when my great-grandfather spit-combed his hair and buttoned his high, stiff collar for the photographer, the most ancient vintage Model T Ford in existence was two years old. The Wright Brothers' flight at Kitty Hawk was only seven years in the past, and pilots were just beginning to explore the possibility of flying at night. Edison's electric lights were still fairly exotic technology that great-grandpa might have been more likely to have read about (by gas light) than to have owned.

On that day his son, my grandfather, who would later command a small aircraft carrier in World War II, was a young child. Looking at that picture, I couldn't help thinking of all the brushes with the world my great-grandfather had experienced up to the day that picture was taken, and all that he still had ahead of him.

Later that same afternoon my 30 year-old son emailed me a picture of himself standing next to his new truck. Aside from the pose and the clothes being quite a bit less formal, and the fact that the image reached me ninety seconds after it was shot instead of the nine weeks it would have taken in great-grandpa's time, the story I saw was pretty much the same.

And it made me think back to when I was the same age, and my son was just cutting his first teeth. I would have just bought a brand new IBM PC, with the optional second floppy drive, an incredibly cool 13" deluxe monitor that could display letters made up of glowing green dots on a black background, and a price tag that some small countries could afford. I passed on the 300 baud modem that could "transmit an entire page in less than ten minutes," because nobody really needs that kind of technological horsepower.

At about that time I read a wild science fiction-ish article about the idea of portable "cellular" phones that you could carry around with you wherever you wanted to go, and every member of the family would have a personal phone number.

Yeah, that's totally going to happen.

The point is, a lot of cool stuff comes along in the course of a lifetime. In the 1950s, when I was a little kid living in Hawaii and our family wanted to go to the mainland to visit, we would climb aboard a giant state of the art propeller-driven Pan Am Strato Clipper for the 8 hour flight from Honolulu to Los Angeles.

I remember the first time I saw a television show in "living color" at the home of a wealthy friend. Even better, I can still feel the excitement of the day my dad brought home our first color TV, a steel box roughly the size of the Space Shuttle Hangar painted to look like it was made out of some sort of wood the color of Marilyn Monroe's hair, and housing a fifteen inch (diagonal measure) screen bursting with all the hues of Walt Disney's creative genius.

A few years later I watched live television coverage of guys walking on the moon.

Just like my other two books – *Bikes, Docks & Slush Nuggets* and *Angels, Chimps & Tater Mitts* – this book is a fairly random collection of a bunch of the interesting things that have come my way over the sixty-plus years I've been knocking around the planet. I'm not sharing this stuff with you because I think my life is especially great or even unique. In fact, what I really hope is that most of my stuff reminds you of your own stuff.

And if it does, then that's some good stuff.

Enjoy!

Now & Then

When I was a kid I had a sort-of girlfriend called Catnip Catie. Her name came from the fact that she always kept her personal supply of Whacky Wonder Weed hidden in her cat's toys. Mind you, this was back in the olden days, before you could get a Prescription for legal Whacky Wonder Weed to treat your case of Restless Leg Syndrome.

I met Catie working in the hospital, where she was a Licensed Practical Nurse and I was a Certified Bedpan Technologist. She was also an artist, so she painted peace signs, and flowers, and variations on those cool Keep On Truckin' cartoon guys on my guitar. She lived in a very colorful little Catie-decorated house trailer parked out in a field behind an old gas station.

Catie didn't turn out to be a huge part of my life. I knew her for a couple of years, then we drifted our separate ways. But sometimes, forty years later, I like to just shut my eyes, and drift back, and hang out for a while in Catie's trailer, inhaling the scent of her patchouli, and her paint, and fresh coffee, and last week's bacon, all laced with just a hint of Whacky Wonder Weed and kitty litter.

It's like that for me - I take little trips back in time to visit vacation spots in my memory.

If I like, I can go back and cruise Bonnie Doone's with my friends in my first car, a 1961 Buick LeSabre. This thing was a rusty behemoth we called the Big Bright Green Pleasure Machine. We regularly used the BBGPM to sneak kids into the drive-in movie, since it had a trunk big enough for four guys - or up to six girls, since girls don't take up all that much space.

Or I can revisit one of those Saturday night brainstorms with my buddies, toward the end of an evening when we were trying to think of a convincing story we could tell our parents to explain why we are all going to spend the night at Tony's house. Of course, we were going to stay at Tony's house because his parents were in Chicago, and we had each polished off enough cans of Pabst Blue Ribbon to make it more or less suicidal to go home.

I can close my eyes and find myself sitting by the fireplace on that first blind date with Nan, playing my guitar and singing her a cheesy John Denver song after a long day of wandering around every possible point of interest in Ann Arbor, amazed that this is what it feels like to find the love of my life, and wondering what spending the next six or seven decades with her is going to be like.

Or I can go back and strut around the streets of downtown Plymouth, Michigan wearing a huge "It's A Boy" button featuring a picture of a little pink newborn lizard named Patrick, passing out bubble gum cigars and knowing that no man anywhere in the world could ever possibly be as proud and happy as I was at that moment.

I occasionally wish that I could physically go back and actually relive some of those times. It would even be kind of fun to once again wipe that little "surprise fountain" out of my eyes; you know, the one you get when you are just a little too casual or too slow changing your little boy's diaper.

OK well, maybe not so much that.

But if I really think it through, I know that I'm really a lot better off where I am right now. For one thing, in most ways I'm a whole lot smarter than I used to be.

Better yet, I just naturally move quite a bit more slowly now, so whenever I turn out to be just as stupid as I ever was, I slide into the inevitable whirlwind of trouble at a much more leisurely pace. This means that I always have plenty of time to duck and minimize the collateral damage.

I think the best way to understand how life really works is to realize that "now" is made up of all the "then" that has come along over the course of all these years that stretch from... well, from then to now. In other words, when I add it all up, I'm glad to find myself right here where I am.

After all, the best part about being here is where I've been.

Paddle to the Tavern

I am the proud owner of a Paddle Boat.

A Paddle Boat is a small lake-going craft that appeals to guys like me who shrugged off that last remaining shred of self-respect the first time we made the decision to wear dockers, flip flops, and an Aerosmith t-shirt to the mall. The only other people who really like them are young children who, face it, never had any sense of dignity to begin with.

Paddle boats come in a variety of sizes and configurations, but they all have three things in common:

1. They float (more or less).

2. You propel them through the water by pedaling like a three-year-old on a floating (more or less) tricycle.

3. The odds are pretty good that your wife will

not want to be seen paddle-boating around on the lake with you.

I'm willing to admit that my paddle boat would probably be considered even dorkier than most. A lot of them are low-slung and sleek (if you consider a sort of rectangular pudding tub with bucket seats and a paddle on the back "sleek"). These modern craft are aerodynamically designed to deal with speeds of up to 0.0003 knots.

Let's take a time out for a learning moment; a "knot" (pronounced "not") is a unit of speed slightly faster than an "mph" (pronounced "mfffff"). This relates to the term "Nautical Mile," which is 1.15078 regular miles. Nautical miles originated with the early sailors, who came up with quite a bit of weird stuff like this, probably because they spent all their time out in the middle of the ocean playing with their sextants and drinking rum.

My paddle boat is pretty much the opposite of low-slung and sleek. It consists of a straight-backed wooden bench that sits about four feet above the water on small aluminum pontoons, with side-by-side pedals and a steering-stick thingie in the middle. Tied to the dock alongside our regular pontoon boat, The Party Barge, it looks like a floating (more or less) Mini-Me.

The word "floating" is always kind of theoretical when we're talking about my paddle boat because one of the pontoons leaks a bit. This gives it a sort of rakish list to port - which means "left" (you can also blame this on the sextants and rum).

All the wood looks like it was recycled from the original picnic table at the Alamo, the one that has Davy Crockett's name carved on it. The pedals squeak because the bearings wore out when Truman was President. The rudder is so loose that steering is really just an abstract concept.

And I would not part with that little paddle boat for all the floating (more or less) tricycles in the world.

It once belonged to Harold, my late neighbor and surrogate father. He used it mostly for fishing, operating on the theory that in a boat without a motor he could just sort of sneak up on herds of unsuspecting bluegills. I never bothered to point out that when those squeaky pedals were going around you could hear him all the way to Georgian Bay.

Harold bought the paddle boat from some folks on the other side of the lake. Over the course of that winter he painted the ancient wood with redwood stain, stuffed some grease into where the bearings used to be, and decided that a little bit of water in one of the pontoons actually gave the thing character. Then he enjoyed it completely until the day came, toward the end of his life, when he could no longer safely make it down the dock to use it.

So tonight I'll hop on that paddle boat and head down the shore to the Tavern, where I can take a moment and hoist a pint to Harold. And I'll smile at the memory of the old guy out there on the lake, squeaking back and forth across the bluegill beds with a fly rod in one hand and a can of beer in the other, thinning out the fish population.

And listing to port.

In the Middle of the Mall

Not too long ago I tagged along with a friend to visit the Apple Store. I wanted to get a peek at the latest iPad model, which as we all know represents the future of human communication. The new one comes complete with Bluetooth, WiFi, 4G connectivity, a video camera, a GPS navigational system, and an ice cube maker.

When you're in the Apple Store you can tell it's the Future, because everything is really, really white - especially the people who work there, who have clearly not seen any sort of sunlight since the first Bush administration.

On the way to the Apple Store we had to pass through the Mall, where the Future happens to be located. I have not been in any sort of Mall for quite a few years, since I only buy clothes in odd-numbered decades, and then only from the

Salvation Army Fashion Superstore, so I was in for a few surprises.

Apparently at some point since my last Mall visit, the people who decide how to best serve the Mall-Visiting Public came to the conclusion that our overall shopping experience would be better if we just had tribes of Visigoth marauders posted at strategic locations throughout the central concourse, to pillaging passing shoppers. These barbarian encampments are called "Kiosks."

Kiosks are little islands of Crap-For-Sale, staffed by apparently foreign-born people who have too many teeth and not enough tattoos to work the Tilt-A-Whirl ride at the county fair. They are trained professionals, thoroughly coached in the latest and most sophisticated customer service techniques, such as grabbing your arm, twisting it behind your back, and delivering a smooth and persuasive sales pitch something like;

"Hey Sport! You can need getting some bling for on your cell phone! Have looks at swell covers what I got for you right over here!"

The variety of Crap-For-Sale available in these Kiosks is pretty impressive. In addition to cell phone bling, you can get your hair straightened by a guy holding a steel dildo heated to the temperature of molten lava. You can get your face "threaded," which is a process in which an Indian woman (the kind with a dot on her forehead, not the kind with a Casino in her family) rips unwanted hairs out of your skin, for some reason using a long piece of dental floss.

You can buy "Dippin' Dots," a special ice cream treat chilled to -70 degrees F, just cold enough to crack your teeth and flash-freeze your uvula (that's the little punching bag thing that hangs over the back of your tongue and lets you say words like, "Rrrrrrrrrrrrrrrrrrrruffles").

There is a guy selling little remote-controlled helicopters, which he demonstrates by performing intricate aerial maneuvers, looping, soaring, and landing gently on the forehead of a woman in the next Kiosk over, who considers it a welcome distraction from getting hairs ripped out of her skin with dental floss. The salesman assures you that the helicopter is, "...real sturdy, like tank, so ain't no way you can gonna break it."

The helicopter lasts exactly as long as it takes you to get it home to your living room, start it up, and let your child fly it to three feet of altitude, at which point it bursts into flames and crashes into your La-Z-Boy.

There is a flooring salesman who demonstrates his product by throwing you to the ground and kneeling on the back of your head, giving you an opportunity to closely examine his product until you sign the check and schedule the installation. Then there is the Jesus Kiosk, where you can sit with a true believer and pray for deliverance from the brutal tyranny of a president who wants health care for poor people.

After I got home from the Mall with my frostbitten uvula and extinguished the fire in my La-Z-Boy, I got to thinking about how I myself might be able to Make Millions in Mall Kiosk Marketing. After careful research on the Internet, enhanced by a six-pack or so of Molson Canadian research-enhancer, I made a list of ideas. Here are a few of the best ones I've come up with so far:

"Mainly Medical" - This would be a kiosk where you could get a tonsillectomy, an appendectomy, and a creditcardectomy, all in the privacy and comfort of a folding lawn chair just outside the entrance to Banana Republic.

"Dr. Doug" - Similar in concept to Mainly Medical, where a guy in a trench coat performs a thorough breast exam and shoots your mammogram with his bling-enhanced cell phone camera.

"Proctology Plaza" - I'm pretty sure you get the idea by now.

"Tweezers Mania" - The Mall's finest selection of Tweezers, Tweezers Caddies, and other Tweezers-related products. Maybe you could even bring in your personal Tweezers from home and get them sharpened "While-U-Wait."

"Weasel World" - All things weasel.

"Staple Station" - Not, as you might think, a place to serve a very special subset of your office supply needs, but the newest trend in Body Art. It's just the thing for those young avant-garde Mall-goers who find having their foreheads pop-riveted to their shin bones just too darned wimpy.

OK, so I'm sure I haven't come close to exhausting the possibilities here. If you have a great idea for a new and better way to pillage Mall shoppers, send it to mike@learnedsofar.com.

The Visigoths are standing by.

The Gospel According to St. Pauli Girl

Beer is living proof that God loves us and wants us to be happy.   - Benjamin Franklin

There are only three things you really need to tackle any home improvement project - a hammer, a friend who knows which end of it to hang on to, and a six pack. - Me

From time to time in this column, I have mentioned the word, "beer." The context is usually something like, "The engineering summit consisted of examining the baffling pile of what we assumed contained all the stuff we were going to need, grunting at each other, and gesturing with our beer bottles."

In response to this, I sometimes hear from readers with comments like, "We really enjoy your column, and think that you are the funniest person who ever lived, but it seems like you drink an awful lot of beer. We have children, you know."

OK, aside from the "funniest person who ever lived" part, this confuses me. First, like most guys, I can't see how anyone could consider "a lot of beer" to be in any way "awful." Second, I am just mentioning beer in my column, not actually swilling it on a public street corner with my pants around my ankles, shuffling in circles and singing, "Polly Wolly Doodle."

And as for your children, rest assured that I am not in any way trying to lead them down the path to certain ruin. That's your job as a parent.

As you might have guessed from the epigrams above, beer lore is woven throughout the history of mankind. According to the Book of Genesis, Noah's provisions for the Ark included beer, although most Bible historians agree that he was probably really good about not tossing the empty cans overboard.

In about 55 BC the Roman legions introduced beer to Northern Europe. Led by Roman General Marcus Labaticus, these troops befriended the little-known "Pretzel" tribe in present-day Germany, and thus were able to conquer the entire region with nothing more than a couple of fist fights in the parking lot.

In 1492, Columbus found Indians making beer from corn and black birch sap. Sensing a marketing opportunity, the explorer set the tribe up in a brick building with big copper vats and $15 hamburgers, inventing the first brewpub. This establishment, unfortunately named, "Yellow-Bear-Stream-In-Woods Brew Haus," has since faded completely from most of the history books.

As the Pilgrims sailed up the Atlantic Coast in 1620, they realized that their beer supplies were running low. Mistaking Plymouth Rock for a 7-Eleven, they immediately landed and spent their first harsh winter in the new world foraging in vain for Slim Jims.

In 1909, Teddy Roosevelt brought five hundred gallons of beer along with him on safari to Africa. While the expedition failed to bring home a lion, they did bag a cow, a donkey, two squirrels, and a "Yield" sign, plus they slightly wounded Roosevelt's personal chef, Reneé.

There are some countries in the world today in which children are virtually raised on beer, drinking it pretty much from the day they are weaned from their mothers. While I don't really condone this, I admit it makes a certain amount of sense to go ahead and let the tykes have a little fun, considering just what it is they're leaving behind.

So there you have it - beer. I enjoy it. Most of my friends enjoy it. Moses, Shakespeare, and Yogi Berra enjoyed it. As a wise man (probably) once said: "Without beer I could live another 40 years. Buy why the heck would I want to?"

Cheers!

Smart Phone

I just upgraded my mobile phone.

First off, I'd like to say that I didn't really want to. I was really happy with my old phone; his name was "Phone." I could use Phone to make calls. I could use him to receive calls. He even had a cool digital clock so I would know when it was time to make or receive a call.

Phone also had a bunch of ultra-modern features. He had a directory of all my friends built in so that whenever I could figure out how to get to the directory, Phone would go ahead and dial people for me. The people that Phone called were usually not the people I had intended to talk to, but over the years I found that I kind of enjoyed that element of surprise.

Phone had built into his back a pretty good camera, which I used from time to time to take pictures of the change in my pocket. Or my thumb. And he had a microscopic keyboard, so that whenever someone sent me a text message like this:

"Hey! How are you?"

... I could just snap open that little keyboard and use my thumbs to nimbly type out a reply:

"lgi uh dfov, to the lajniak! ;-}"

So even though I knew that my mobile company was ready and willing to give me a new phone for free, I had every intention of hanging on to good old Phone for a while longer. He did pretty much everything I needed, and he had become my friend.

Then a few days ago, while I was out on the boat, I felt that I should completely eliminate any chance of getting Phone wet, so I popped him into a handy cup holder. As it turned out, I had not taken into account the inch of rain water in the bottom of that cup holder. I could almost hear Phone's dying words, just as I might have typed them out for him on his keyboard:

"Ygly blark norfni... :-("

So I went down to the cell phone kiosk to pick out a new phone. The guy there, who could not have been more than about eleven years old and yet clearly knew everything there is to know about every cell phone ever made, told me that it was my lucky day - I was eligible to get a free "Smart Phone."

I'm here to tell you that the phone he fixed me up with is very smart indeed. The new phone's name is "Kierkegaard."

Kierkegaard is a bit more technologically advanced than old Phone was, in much the same way that a nuclear reactor is more technologically advanced than a kitchen match. I can make him do all kinds of amazing feats by downloading and installing things called "Apps." As far as I can tell, "App" is short for "App-arently you are kind of bored and need to kill some time loading some really crazy crap into your phone."

When you look at Kierkegaard all you see is four small buttons and a blank glass screen. This is deceptive. I have discovered that if I hit the right button, that screen comes alive with little pictures of things, like rain clouds, and cartoon speech balloons, along with dozens of completely indecipherable things that nevertheless look really cool.

If I poke around on the pictures on the screen for a while I can show movies, browse Web sites, check on eBay listings, read my emails, check out the latest weather radar, update my Facebook, navigate precisely to a used car dealership in Butte, Montana, study a map of the sky that has every star, planet and constellation clearly labeled, and look up dirty words in a handy unabridged dictionary.

What you don't see anywhere on Kierkegaard is any sort of key pad you could use to dial a phone call. OK, every now and then, if I happen to push the right sequence of buttons and hold my mouth just right, a picture of a keypad appears on the screen. And touching various places on this picture actually does sometimes work to make phone calls.

More often, though, I find myself using the handy "Voice Dialing" feature. I simply speak a name into the phone, and Kierkegaard goes ahead and calls someone whose name sounds vaguely similar to the one I spoke.

I admit that I kind of enjoy carrying a phone around that is smarter than I am. Even though I'm still a little unclear about how to answer an incoming call, I think I will enjoy the years of companionship that little Kierkegaard and I have ahead of us, debating over the concept of objective reality as it affects principles of theistic existentialism.

At least until I drop him into a cup holder full of water.

I Can't Wait to Be a Grandpa

Do you remember when you were a kid and you just finished doing something spectacularly stupid, and your mom would say, "You just wait, Buster. Some day you'll have children of your own, and then you'll get yours..."

As with most things, my mother was right. My son spent the better part of his childhood doing heroic duty to her memory, picking up and channeling every one of my childhood sins so that retribution for my own evil deeds could wash back over me in a giant dose of Kiddie Karma.

Now that my son is grown and married, I've decided that I'm going to raise the ante.

You see, as parents it was our job to teach our kids to say, "Thank you" and to keep their pants pulled up when we had company. We had to convince them that it is generally a good idea to flush the toilet. It was our responsibility to mold them into future doctors, lawyers, astronauts, politicians, armed robbers, or televangelists.

A grandpa is free to be nothing more than a kindly old coot with an endless lap and a bottomless wallet.

And I have come to believe that we can use our special status to get the ultimate revenge on our sons and daughters. Like graying and slightly arthritic Doctor Frankensteins, we can lovingly shape our grandchildren into perfect little monsters.

Here are five simple ideas to get you started:

• Take them to the zoo. Gently explain to them that they could have a zebra of their very own, if only Mommy and Daddy weren't so mean.

• Always show up bearing gifts. Start with something like a slide whistle or a tambourine, and work your way up from there. Your grandkids will never forget their first snare drum.

• Once you've exhausted the world of high-decibel entertainment, and the grandkids are old enough that you don't have to worry about them choking on small things, you can move on to toys with thousands of components, each one small enough to go unnoticed but large enough to detonate the old Hoover. With careful shopping, you should be able to find Legos that will blend perfectly with virtually any carpet.

• Any time the grandkids are with you, keep the chocolate flowing; you always want to bring them home talking fast and grinding their teeth. Hershey Kisses are particularly ideal for this, since they have to be handled a lot and will tend to get nicely smeared on hands, faces, in hair, behind ears, and occasionally over every square inch of a sibling.

• To follow up on this last idea, before you send them home you should stuff their backpacks with treats "for the road." Here again, Hershey's Kisses are ideal, with an added bonus that the little foil wrappers will end up scattered like shrapnel all over your son or daughter's home.

And so forth. The main thing is to always be alert for opportunities to sow the seeds of discontent. For example, if you should happen to notice the grandkids watching a motocross on TV, simply drop a casual comment like, "You know, I really think every kid should have a dirt bike." Just stay sharp and be creative - the possibilities are endless.

Now I will admit that all of this is speculative - we don't actually have any grandchildren of our own yet, despite all the charts, diagrams, and instruction sheets I've sent to my son over the years.

And, now that I read it over, it seems like this column might explain a lot.

Confessions of a (New) Facebookaholic

Hi. I'm Mike, and I'm a Facebookaholic.

I discovered Facebook not too long ago, at the suggestion of some of my creative writing students. "It's great," they would tell me, "you can do all kinds of stuff."

"And what kind of 'stuff' might we be talking about here?" I would ask, in my very best imitation of Mrs. Gadomski, the severe and ancient (probably twenty years younger than I am now) high school Latin teacher who inspired me to strive for greatness as an educator, and who triggered many hours of speculation among most of us students as to what kind of man would be at all interested in being "Mr. Gadomski."

My present-day gang of young Shakespeares are every bit as persistent as they are creative, and they eventually convinced me to give Facebook a try. The way Facebook works, you find and link up with Friends through Friend Requests.

Within minutes of signing up I started receiving Friend Requests from all sorts of people, and in many cases I had at least a vague idea who they were. Not wanting to seem unsociable, I accepted the Friend Requests from the people I could identify, and from all my "new Friends" too.

After taking a closer look and weeding out all the "new" Friends who had names like "Hornee McOnlinehooker," I was ready to dive in and be a Facebook Guy.

The first thing you have to do as a Facebook Guy is post your Status. You just find the little box toward the top of your Home Page that says "What are you doing now?" and you fill it in. Luckily for all of us, it is pretty rare for anybody to answer that question with, "Trying to think of something to write in this little Facebook box."

Instead, people tend to come up with answers yielding deep insights into their emotional states. You see Status comments like (these are real), "Jessica is orange juice orange juice orange juice orange juice," or "Alana is RAAAAAAH."

Every time one of your Friends posts an update to their Status it appears on your Home Page. This gives you interesting, if cryptic and occasionally frightening, minute-to-minute insight into how each of their lives is unfolding, often with a little bit more information than you were really hoping for: "Larry is coffee, English muffin, and explosive diarrhea."

You can also post your own pictures and movies to Facebook. This gives users a chance to share their most exuberantly joyful, deeply personal, or just plain silly moments with all their friends. Who wouldn't want to see pictures of you at the Halloween party, dressed as a Vietnamese hooker and chugging a keg of beer through a garden hose? Of course, you are also sharing those moments with a few other people - like the woman you have the job interview with next week.

OK, from here on, Facebook starts to get kind of strange.

First, there are all kinds of games you can play. When I joined up, I almost immediately started getting something called "(Lil) Green Patch Requests," which are messages saying that various Friends wanted to send me things like pictures of lilies, pansies, and little cartoon people with cauliflowers and strawberries for hats.

You are apparently supposed to collect these plants and little cartoon people on your screen in a virtual garden. You can re-arrange them, rake them (I have no idea what that's about), or steal rainbows to hang over them, and when squirrels come around you give them nuts. Somehow all of this saves the Rain Forest. Kind of like the Holly Hobby version of Greenpeace.

I've also been kidnapped with crazy purple knockout gas, hit with a snowball, invited to a bunny fight, and received a Pokemon gift of 25 Poke-bucks.

I have no clue what any of this stuff means, which I guess should not be too surprising. Facebook was originally designed as a way for college students to kill time while they are away at school filling their heads with advanced knowledge and their laptops with computer viruses.

Anyway, I guess my addiction to Facebook is not all that bad yet. I don't need it all that much. I mean, I could probably quit any time I want to. Really. No, really. I mean it. Any time I want to.

Or maybe I could just taper off with a couple of shots of Twitter.

Next time: The Old Folks Invade Facebook

Facebook II – Attack of the Online Geezers

Last week I wrote about my new-found fondness for the popular social networking site Facebook. This is an online resource originally designed for college students, a virtual world where the young scholar could post photographs of her best friend, wearing a pair of men's boxer shorts and a hot pink Gap sweatshirt, passed out in a bathtub with a picture of a penis drawn in lipstick on her forehead.

Unfortunately, those halcyon days of artistic expression may now be threatened by a group of Net denizens who are gradually infiltrating every corner of Facebook. I am, of course, referring to myself and all my friends.

Yes, once an online playground defined by images of bikini-clad undergrad girls on Spring Break sipping Piña Coladas in the pool in Cancun with Tecate-drunk undergrad guys looking as if they can't quite believe their luck, Facebook is now home to book clubs, forty-year high school reunion committees, and hemorrhoid awareness groups.

How could this happen?

I have discovered that you can pretty much trace the whole thing back to Chelsea Goldfarber, a university freshman from McCook, Nebraska who got homesick and invited her mom, Gloria, to join Facebook - just so they could keep "in touch."

Gloria, who is a past president of the McCook Junior High School PTO and a born organizer, immediately called everyone in her phone directory who owned a computer and talked them into joining up. She quickly built up a network of middle-aged women all over McCook and the surrounding suburbs (you know; Perry, Red Willow, Indianola, Culbertson...) posting albums of their Shih Tzu's and forming Johnny Depp fan groups.

The word was out. Before long, a tsunami of older users from all around the world had swept through Facebook. Now all those undergrads in bikinis are being elbowed aside by priceless photos of grandchildren making pancakes.

So where is the downside of all this? Clearly we Baby Boomers bring with us a rich tapestry of insights derived from our years of life experience. I mean, we can remember gas for thirty cents a gallon, Richard Nixon's sweaty upper lip, and even the strangely interesting nationally-televised changes in Annette's Mouseketeer T-shirt as we all got our first introduction to the concept of puberty on the Mickey Mouse Club.

The problem is that anything you post for your friends can be seen by all your friends. And kids, the first thing a doting parent is going to want to do when they join Facebook is become your friend. Good luck turning down that particular Request.

And of course this means that every time someone flags a picture of you drinking Jaeger Bombs from an aircraft refueling funnel, your parents will see it. I'm just guessing that, unless your folks are the kind who bought you a monogrammed beer bong for your birthday, this might not be a good thing for you.

I'm not sure what the solution is here. Personally, I like using Facebook to catch up with friends I've not seen since Old Sweaty-Lip was in the White House (for you younger folks, that would be Richard Nixon), and I won't be giving it up any time soon. And on the other side, the young Facebookers seem to be pretty well dug in too.

My nephew told me his plan was that, if any of us geezers get too "opinionated or uppity," he could just post scans of old Polaroids of us in our lime green polyester leisure suits and platform shoes. I had to break it to him that his idea would probably not work, since we all think we looked pretty hot back then.

Maybe Facebook could provide users with an age-sensitive automatic Fogy Flag. This would allow younger users to set up and automatically direct any of us Fogies to a "parent-safe" version of their Facebook, containing nothing but shots of them studying the dioramas at the Natural History Museum.

Oh well, time will tell how it will all work out. In the meantime I'm going to wrap this up and hop back over to Facebook, just in case anyone's grandkids have managed to work their way up to waffles.

Eddie's Choice

"So what's on your minds, guys?" It was a pretty open-ended question to ask a group of incarcerated teenage boys, and the range of answers I got pretty much lived up to my expectations;

"Eatin' pizza!"

"Girls!"

"Eatin' pizza with girls!"

There were a few other topics that I am probably better off leaving to your imagination.

Josh White, Jr. and I were working our way through the first session of a new idea we were developing, helping severely troubled young people explore some of their deepest feelings by writing and performing folk and blues songs. At the time we were calling the program "Project Roots," referring to the fact that traditional folk and blues, or "roots music," forms the foundation on which all other American music is built.

On that day we were not really sure where to start, because nobody else had ever tried to do exactly what we were doing. I had been running creative writing workshops at this facility for nearly two years and some of these boys had been in at least one of my groups. They all knew me. This was a big advantage, since I had already had a chance to earn their trust - and trust is something that never comes easy for these kids.

So we were throwing ideas around and I was sorting through them, looking for something that might suggest a song. Then one of the boys said, "I'm getting out pretty soon. I don't really know what's going to happen after that." In a group of kids who have been locked up, some of them for a pretty big chunk of their young lives, I had found this a fairly common source of conversation.

But listening to them on that day, I began to realize that they were really talking about choices. You see, when you're locked up, "The System" makes all your decisions for you - when to wake up, when to eat, when to sleep, when to read, even when to visit the toilet. Most of these kids were working hard to truly come to grips with the idea that they were locked up because of their own bad choices.

So what was gnawing away at them was the idea that they would someday be making choices again, some of them for the first time in years. And for most of them, their next bad choice would land them in prison, for real and maybe forever.

I jumped on it. "Let's write some blues," I said, "about a guy getting out of this place."

We created a character and named him "Eddie." Then, working through every word as a team, we began to tell Eddie's story;

Eddie's gone tonight at midnight,
They're about to kick him out that door.
He's got a sweatshirt, shoes and blue jeans,
A plan, and nothing more.

And we wrote a chorus;

In and out of locked doors,
Same old song and dance.
This time's got to be different,
Ain't gonna be another chance.

As the story goes, Eddie heads down to the bus stop, where his brother is going to pick him up. When he arrives, there is a "gnarled and dusty man" waiting for him. The old man tells him,"I've got some things to say, and I've been savin' you a seat."

Eddie is not real interested in the ramblings of this drifter, but the old man persists;

35

You know, that ride that's coming for you,
You been in that car before.
You might have won some battles
But you're bound to lose the war.

And later, after having Eddie tell him that, "Until you've been locked up, you'll never know just what it's like;"

The old man smiles and says,
"I walked some miles in your shoes
I played it all the hard way.
Now all I have is blues."

What the kids decided, but did not spell out in the song is that the old man is one possible Eddie, from years down the line, come back to deliver a warning.

Here is how the boys wrapped up the song they decided to call "Eddie's Choice:"

Eddie's ride pulls up,
And he starts to walk away.
But with his hand on the car door,
He stops and looks the old man's way -
And he says;
"In and out of locked doors,
Same old song and dance.
This time's got to be different,
Ain't gonna be another chance."

For these young men maybe, just maybe, this time really can be different.

Lost Voices was initially developed as "Project Roots" at the WJ Maxey Boys Training School in Whitmore Lake Michigan and the Adrian Girls Training Center in Adrian, MI with funding from the National Endowment for the Arts through the Michigan Humanities Council and the Michigan Council for Arts and Cultural Affairs, along with the Northfield Township Library. Lost Voices is an independent 501(c)3 formed in 2007 to continue and expand this work nationwide.

You can get more information about Lost Voices or make a donation online at lostvoices.org.

The Dawn Of a
(Sort Of) New Dock

Well, it's that time of year again. The ice dam in the driveway has been replaced by a glob of nearly composted leaves from last autumn, I've extracted the last of the season's Slush Nuggets from the bushes, and the First Robin of Spring has become a dreamy smile of well-fed satisfaction on the face of the neighbor's cat.

It's time to put The Dock back out in the lake!

I've written about The Dock before. To review, it's basically a collection of mismatched metal poles and wooden sections that we have cobbled together over the course of the past fifteen years. Just picture a majestic but run-down old barn, with all the wood a deeply weathered gray, bent and warped under the weight of untold seasons of hardship and honest toil. Only it's a dock.

I inherited most of The Dock when I moved in here. The guy I bought the house from took his nice dock with him to his new place, and he scavenged this one just so there would be something in the water when he sold the house. I'm sure he figured he was just doing me a temporary favor, and that only an idiot would try to keep the thing together and use it for fifteen years.

So far, we've got fifteen years out of The Dock. To replace the sections that actually disintegrated while we were walking on them, we built some additional ones from scratch, painstakingly copying the old ones so that they were absolutely identical in every way, aside from the length, width, height, weight, color and the occasional beer koozie inadvertently screwed to the planking.

To get The Dock further out into the lake we needed to add more sections. We got these handed down by friends who were buying new docks of their own and decided to donate the old stuff to me, since none of it was good enough to be used for firewood.

The bottom line is, The Dock consists of a pretty much random variety of widths, supports and connections, which means that attaching one section to the next can be kind of like trying to figure out how to hook a railroad freight car to the trailer hitch on a Mazda.

So last year, once we had the Dock basically functioning we decided to take a picture of the completed assembly to serve as a sort of blueprint for future docks. This would spare us the many hours of standing in the lake in our waders, drinking beer and designing clever engineering solutions, all the while wishing there was an easy way to go to the bathroom when you're wearing waders.

After many hours of searching for the picture (fortunately you don't have to wear waders to do that), I found it and examined last year's Dock. Along with the vital technical information, I also noticed that the thing was sort of crooked.

I can be more specific. In some past years our Dock, when viewed from a distance, would seem to form a curve or a gentle "S" shape. The one in this picture more or less spelled out, in a kind of uneven and pointy-edged script, the word "wünderbar."

Now while it was kind of cool in a way to have a dock that spoke German, I was more than a little bit embarrassed when I realized that the "umlaut" was actually two ducks who, having become disoriented by all the weaving from side to side as they walked the dock, and because of some pretty severe leveling problems, had toppled into the water.

I decided right then and there that this year The Dock was going to be as straight and level as I could possibly get it. If those ducks fell off this year, it would be because they had been dipping their little beaks in some boater's Jaeger Bombs.

So, when my friend Tom showed up to tackle The Dock with me, I had my Craftsman® Laser Level all mounted on a tripod and ready to use.

Next time – My friend Tom also has no idea how to use a Craftsman® Laser Level.

The Dawn Of a (Sort Of) New Dock Part II – Laser Tales

At the end of last week's action-packed episode, we left our heroes, Tom and Mike, staring thoughtfully at a big heap of alleged dock sections, a fairly strange assortment of poles, augers, and connectors, some other stuff we couldn't quite identify, and one brand new Craftsman® Laser Level.

Important safety tip – don't ever stare thoughtfully at a laser level.

The idea behind our foray into twenty-first century laser technology was that we were planning to be a little more meticulous putting the dock together than we have in years past, when the contours of our finished work served as a sort of idealized prototype for the ride designers at Cedar Point. We figured that something that looked as complicated as this little laser thingie had to be good.

I should point out that the only reason I own a laser level is that my son gave it to me for Father's Day a couple of years ago. I have always thought it would be incredibly cool to have my very own laser level, or for that matter anything that had a "laser" involved with it in any way.

You see, when I was a kid lasers were the stuff of science fiction. Mounted in the belly of an Antarian Battle Saucer, they could destroy a continent or blast a Rigelian Mining Frigate clean out of orbit. They were always the weapons of choice for space-suited heroes who needed to deal with the vicious Klenthar Beasts on Alpha Persei Nine.

Then during my first year in college I had an opportunity to visit a laboratory at the University of Notre Dame, where they were conducting ground-breaking research on one of the earliest working lasers. It was a huge, exciting room filled with humming boxes, prisms, mirrors, and grad students charging around in white lab coats and dark goggles.

The end result of all this activity was a thin red beam of light that you could see when you blew smoke across it, zigzagging around the room between all the mirrors and ending up in a tiny dot on a piece of tissue paper. One of the goggle wearers proudly told me that if they could just find a way to boost the power by seven or eight orders of magnitude, they could maybe – just maybe - blow a hole right through that nasty old paper!

At the time I was pretty impressed with how science was catching up with science fiction, even though I recall thinking that these folks were probably at least a couple of research grants away from being able to bring down a charging Klenthar Beast.

In any case, I don't recall any science fiction author ever incorporating into his view of the future the idea that laser technology would some day end up in the key fobs of middle school students, enabling them to hilariously make their friends think that they are being targeted by a sniper.

So here Tom and I sat, looking from the dock heap, to the laser level, to the lake, to the instructions that came with the laser level, and back to the dock heap. We were both wearing our red "Laser Level safety glasses," and we had already lost a fair amount of time marveling over how these glasses made Tom's red truck look yellow. It was time to get down to business.

After carefully putting the instructions back in the carrying case (so we would know where to find them just in case we ever decided to read them), we set up a small tripod to hold the laser level, carefully adjusting it to give us a true reading. Then we invested a couple of beers in a thorough debate over the best strategy for taking laser readings and using them to produce the perfect dock.

Finally, armed with our plan, we put on our waders, grabbed the tripod, and headed out to the water, where we discovered that even with the special glasses, in bright sunshine you can't really see a laser level well enough to do you much good.

Did you know that, with a little creativity, a laser level in a dark room works even better than a laser pointer to drive a cat completely psychotic?

Memorial Day

Memorial day is one of my favorite holidays, and not just because it is one of the first excuses of the new summer season to dress up in shorts, tank tops and flip flops for our ritual orgy of brats and beer in the back yard.

For one thing, it was a pretty darned fine weekend for those of us who like to look at race cars and girls in skimpy outfits. This year, it all started with the Grand Prix of Monaco on Sunday at 8:00 AM (3:00 AM if you prefer not to see your effete European superstars rocketing past the yacht club on tape delay).

While the Formula 1 folks have a seemingly endless supply of beautiful women in micro-miniskirts scattered liberally around every camera shot, one of my favorite parts of any Grand Prix is the interview with the Scandinavian drivers after the race. Their English is always terrific, but they deliver their deadpan speeches in a sort of staccato Nordic monotone that is a masterpiece of elocution. And breath control:

"Well, forsure, westartedoutgood, but wecouldn't catchKimibeforethefirststop, andthenwehadtheproblemwiththetirecompound, butforsure, theteamdidagreatjob togetustothirdplace, and, forsure, wearedisappointed wecouldnotwintoday, butwearehappytogetaplaceonthepodium, andwewill, forsure, buildonthis forthenextrace."

A little later on you have Indianapolis 500, the "Greatest Spectacle in Racing." As a general rule the skirts do not tend to run quite as high on the thigh in central Indiana as they do on the Riviera, but the cars are even faster. And whenever the network has a little time to kill, you get some great bikini shots of Danica Patrick.

I really love the NASCAR event, the Coca-Cola 600. These cars aren't nearly as quick as the ones they drive in Indy or Formula 1 races, but they are fast enough. They are also built so the drivers can do a fair amount of bumping and banging each other around, so a driver trying to work his way through race traffic at 200 miles per hour is just like any of us regular folks trying to make it through the parking lot at Costco.

In fact, one of the biggest draws of NASCAR is that cars are supposed to remind us of the ones we all drive every day - especially those of us who drive cars with decals for headlights and tail lights, run engines with just a little less than 900 horse-power, and are sponsored by Viagra.

The women of NASCAR stand alone - usually with one hip provocatively shoved out to the side. These girls are pretty much walking advertisements for chemically enhanced hair color and surgically enhanced body parts. As of this writing, I have never met a man who had any sort of problem with that.

This year monsoons in Charlotte, North Carolina caused hours of rain delays in the Coca-Cola 600, which gave the network plenty of time to run commercials featuring Danica Patrick unzipping her racing suit.

On Memorial Day here in Detroit, unlike cities like, say, Anaheim, we have an added sports bonus; our Red Wings hockey team is still playing for the Stanley Cup. There is just something really special about sitting back to enjoy a Molson and the smell of sunscreen on an American holiday weekend afternoon, while you watch a bunch of Canadians and Europeans fly around on a big sheet of ice and beat each other senseless.

Of course, there is another meaning to Memorial Day, one that sometimes gets lost in all the roaring engines and balloons and tight t-shirts and – well, balloons. I think it is a good idea to remember that the actual holiday is here to commemorate the men and women who served our country as soldiers, especially those who gave their lives in that service.

I can't help thinking about my father, still in his teens, going into the Army Air Corps during World War II. At an age when the biggest thing on the minds of most of our kids today is how they are going to get their hands on the latest iPhone, he was riding around in the nose of a B-17 heavy bomber, looking down at a devastated planet through a bomb sight.

My father came home after the war and started a family. A lot of his friends did not make it back, just like a lot of my friends never made it back from Vietnam. In both cases, it seems like all those who did were changed forever.

I can't help thinking back through our nation's history about all the friends, and fathers, and mothers, and sons, and daughters, and brothers, and sisters who have left their innocence or their lives behind on battlefields around the world. They were all people who had the courage to step up and accept the job of protecting our country, to do what our leaders told them to do, and if necessary to lay down their lives doing it.

So I hope you enjoyed all the racing, and the girls, and the sun on your Memorial Day just as much as I did. But I also hope you took a few minutes to think about the people who gave up the chance to be here to enjoy it all with us. And next time you see a vet, don't wait until next May to salute them.

They earned it.

Another Special Father's Day

This past weekend was the Summer Solstice, the longest day of the year. Each year thousands of latter day Druids celebrate the first instant of the summer season. They congregate to share, discuss and revel in their spiritual awakening at sacred places like southern England's Stonehenge, or east Ann Arbor's Denny's.

With the Solstice falling on Saturday this year, there was a pretty aggressive Summer Solstice party here at the lake, as measured in BBD (Beers Before Dark) units. I didn't actually make it out to join the celebration, but judging from the happy revelers washing up on our beach wearing Jaeger Bomb T-shirts and beatific smiles, it was a big success.

Of course, the other big thing that happened this past weekend was Father's Day. Inspired by the Solstice, I was going to really get into the spirit of the thing and sacrifice a goat in a bonfire, mainly so I could wear my brand new barbecue apron imprinted, "You Don't Have To Be A Pagan To Cook Here, But It Helps." It turns out sacrificial goats are in pretty short supply around our house, so I had to settle for chuck ribs on the grill.

Father's Day has always been a fun day for me. I typically plan to lounge around and watch ball games and NASCAR, enjoy a phone call from my son, and maybe even rack up a few BBD of my own. Oddly enough, other than the wonderful phone call, it never seems to work out that way.

For some reason I always seem to end up getting uncharacteristically inspired to get things done around the house. This year it was cutting the grass and sucking flood water out of the carpet in the basement. And I actually enjoyed it.

Happy times!

Even before our son was born my wife began giving me cards on Father's Day, based on the hypothesis that I was father to whatever collection of fuzzy critters we happened to have living with us at the time. This has continued throughout the years, as we raised our slightly less fuzzy critter and put him through college.

In the way of a gift my wife also picks me up a neat little assortment of what she considers to be "dad" things. In the early days I would get something like a sleeve of floating golf balls, a testament to my self confidence and my psychological inability to lay up on a long water hole.

This year she got me a box of adhesive bandages (given my enthusiasm for life and my relative lack of physical coordination, I go through a lot of these in a year), a box of Tiger Balm Liniment Pads (arthritis has pretty much taken over for the thrill of trying to coax a three wood shot across the water hazard), and a heavy-duty room deodorizer kit – do I really need to comment on that?

She also got me a t-shirt that has already become my new favorite article of clothing. It has a picture of a 1966 VW Microbus on it, along with a surf board, a ukulele, and some palm trees. Below this scene are the words, "Where It All Began."

It would be difficult to explain why that shirt meant so much to me the instant I saw it; how closely it touches some of my deepest feelings and fondest memories. It has to do with my own father and his prized VW Microbus, and our traditional family trips to the beach on Christmas Day when I was very young and we were living in Hawaii, and my lifelong love affair with music that he kicked off with the gift of a ukulele one of those Christmas mornings such a long time ago.

My father has been gone for almost forty years now. He wasn't around to see my brother and me graduate from college. He never got a hug from either one of his daughters-in-law. He wasn't around to teach any of his grandchildren how to skin a bluegill.

But that shirt is a perfect reminder of how good it was sometimes, back where it all began. We miss you dad. Happy Father's Day.

Hamburgers and International Monetary Policy

Today my wife and I observed one of our family's most hallowed traditions. It's a custom that has transcended generations, unfailingly signaling the end of the long, cold winter and the approach of at least a few days and nights guaranteed to be completely free from wool socks and ChapStick. I'm talking about the First Hamburger of Spring.

Actually, when I sat down to write this column I was planning to discuss President Obama's trip to Europe and the G-20 Conference in London - but then I fired up my barbecue grill, the Enterprise, and I got distracted.

I guess writing about the G-20 would have been all right. While the Conference itself was probably real entertaining, what with all that sparkling conversation about global economic recovery and financial regulatory reforms, I found myself even more intrigued with imagining all the stuff the press didn't cover.

Like, I'd love to have seen some footage of Barack Obama in the after-hours poker game, bluffing French President Nicolas Sarkozy and British Prime Minister Gordon Brown with a pair of threes. Or the President trying to get Chinese President Hu Jintao to stick his fingers into one of those little bamboo Chinese finger traps.

Or Michelle Obama in the powder room with German Chancellor Angela Merkel, trying valiantly to explain the nuances of the American word "badonkadonk."

Of course one of the highlights of the week came when the Obamas met Queen Elizabeth and Prince Phillip. The big news came when Michelle and Her Royal Highness decided to be BFF's, and put their arms around each other. According to Fox News, this was a breach of protocol that was destined to completely destabilize NATO. Pretty much everybody else on the planet, including the Queen, thought it was kind of cute.

But where were the cameras when the Queen first tried out that iPod the Obamas gave her? According to the President's spokespeople, it was loaded with show tunes. I would have given a lot to have seen just a few minutes of Elizabeth II with her ear buds in, krumping to "Jellicle Cats."

A friend of mine mentioned that she couldn't help wondering what the Queen has in that little black purse of hers. That question seemed a little strange to me, until my friend pointed out that no woman carries her purse around inside her own home. Of course, when you live in an 828,818 square foot house, you might want to have some Life Savers, a hankie, a compass, and a pack of saltines along with you any time you venture south of the rumpus room.

So I guess in a lot of ways, the G-20 Conference could have been a pretty interesting topic for a column.

Or if I was a little more sophisticated, I might have been tempted to discuss Michelle taking on Carla Bruni-Sarkozi on the streets of Paris, pitting J. Crew against Christian Dior in a graciously smiling couture smack down. It was a hand shake, a double cheek kiss for the cameras, and then a high-fashion fight to the finish.

But since I don't really know much about global finance, international diplomacy, or any of that high-society stuff, I am probably better off not writing about it. All in all, I'm on much firmer ground when I stick to subjects I totally understand, like standing in front of the grill with a spatula in one hand and a nice cold Molson in the other.

So, to make a long story short, the burgers were delicious.

All About Weddings

A friend just sent me a very cool link to a YouTube video shot at the wedding of a couple named Jill and Kevin. It consists of the wedding party entering the sanctuary of the small Minnesota church. Here's the link: http://bit.ly/mw4ha. As I am writing this, more than seven million people have watched this video.

For my YouTube challenged readers, this is not footage of a bunch of bridesmaids wearing dreamsicle-colored taffeta, stop-stepping along to Mendelssohn's "Wedding March." Instead, the entire wedding party dances down the aisle to the Auto-Tune drenched sound of a popular club song called "Forever," moving with a level of enthusiasm that actually renders the word "dance" a major understatement.

Can you imagine what the reception was like?

It looks to me like Jill and Kevin are off to a pretty good start. I think it's about as good as it gets to see a couple of kids, along with all their friends, relaxing and enjoying the heck out of every minute of their wedding day.

A few laps back in my life I spent some years working as a professional photographer, and I had the opportunity to shoot a number of weddings. In the process, I rarely saw a young couple having anything like the kind of fun that Jill and Kevin had. What I did see, along with the occasional tuxedo clad fist fight and dreamsicle-colored wardrobe malfunction, was a wide assortment of tense grooms, hysterical brides, angry fathers, and tense, hysterical, angry moms.

And I always wondered why these otherwise sane, wonderful people would put themselves through all that turmoil. Maybe it was because of the amount of time and money they and their parents had invested. Maybe it was because they felt the need to make their wedding the "perfect party." Maybe it was because they thought they were obliged to live out a dream with its roots in a story book.

In some cultures the status of the family is determined by the extravagance of the wedding they throw for their children. Of course, in most of the societies that openly admit to this, a good bride will cost the groom's family five cows, a goat, and a new stool for the Summer Hut.

I know some of you might watch this and think that Jill and Kevin's dance was disrespectful of the church. Maybe so. But in the Psalms it says, "Make a joyful noise unto the Lord." And while the Lord might not be a huge fan of Auto-Tune (who is?), you have to admit that the noise certainly was joyful in every sense of the word. I don't recall the Psalms saying anything specific about a "joyful dance," but it seems like moving around a little bit would be a natural extension of that whole "noise" thing.

Thirty-four years ago when Nan and I got married, we were determined to have fun at our wedding. We got hitched in a little stone church near the University of Michigan campus because we liked the looks of the building and enjoyed talking to the pastor. We did it in July during the Ann Arbor Art Fair, a time of year when Ann Arbor is a wonderland of hippies driving micro-busses bursting with hand-tooled belts and ceramic mugs. Nobody wore ties. The reception was a potluck at the home of a friend who had a swimming pool in the yard, where I learned from my brand new niece and nephew how to play "Marco Polo."

I guess some people might say that our little chapel ceremony and potluck were not "special" enough to really count as a great wedding, that it was just an everyday party. Those people might say that the only way to make it a real wedding is to rent tuxedos, shove wedding cake up each other's noses, and do the "Hokey Pokey."

But I have to disagree, because those traditions don't really have anything to do with what makes it all work. To be sure, there is nothing wrong with the "Hokey Pokey" or snorting a little white frosting, or any of the other customs you might like to adopt from the Standard Wedding Play-book. It's your party.

And if, like Jill and Kevin, you want to have a processional that falls somewhere between a dance number from Grease and the Charge of the Light Brigade, I say, "Knock yourself out."

But I think it is important to remember that a wedding is really a very simple concept. It's all about two people who take each other by the hand, look each other in the eye, and then set out together to tackle the most difficult and rewarding adventure of their lives.

An adventure that will last, with a little luck, fot the rest of their lives.

New Perils of Technology

I received a pretty unique voice mail the other day. According to the caller ID it was from a friend who likes to talk almost as much as I do, so I was not all that surprised to see that her message was more than fifteen minutes long.

As I listened to it, though, I was kind of puzzled. She didn't say anything, but I could hear faint sounds of shuffling silverware and stacking dishes. I could also hear my friend's voice, ghostly and distant, singing in the background. After a few minutes of this, I heard keys jangling, a car door slamming, and then a radio playing - with more of that weird, haunting, far-away singing. I mean "weird" in the best possible way, Leah. Really I do.

Actually, it didn't take too long to figure out what was going on. This was simply a natural outgrowth of our modern times, a reflection of the complex interaction between humans and our own rapidly changing technological world. It was a manifestation of our society's struggle between our finest creations and the Almighty for possession of our very souls.

In other words, I had been butt-dialed.

Butt-dialing happens when you sit on your cell phone, and the roll of Mentos that are crammed in the same pocket with it pushes the "Send" button. The consequences of butt-dialing can be fairly unnerving. My own first experience with it involved standing in a completely silent elevator full of strangers, thinking that I was having a stroke or some sort of hallucination when I heard the faint, reedy voice of my wife shouting, "Mike! Mike!" from somewhere south of my belt.

Luckily, butt-dialed calls usually go to people you know well enough that you have them programmed into your phone's speed dial. In my case, every one of these people are fully aware that I am an idiot, and are prepared to forgive me for the call.

I did hear about one guy a few years ago, who dropped his pants in a men's room stall in Baltimore and his Mentos managed somehow to dial the White House. In less than an hour the Secret Service had him in custody, questioning him for nearly two weeks about directing "threatening noises" toward President Bush. Apparently Karl Rove had him turned over to the CIA, and the last word we had, he was living in special "guest" accommodations in Bulgaria.

Well, that's what I heard.

Butt-dialing was pretty much unknown when I was young. For one thing, "dialing" involved using a sort of "dial," where you stuck your finger in a specific hole in a plastic disc (we called it the "dial"), then turned the disc to the little stopper thingie, then listened to the "dial" click its way back to the starting point. I may be wrong, but I'm pretty sure that's why we call it "dialing" today. If you sat on one of these phones, all you would get was a bruise.

Then along came a revolutionary technology in the 1960s known as Touch Tone Dialing. We all thought that this was pretty cool. You just poked the buttons on your touch tone phone, and it placed a call. The best thing was that each button played a different musical note, so you could play songs on your phone. The most harassed person in America was Velma Ridley of Roanoke, Virginia, whose touch tone phone number was "Yankee Doodle."

Still, if you sat on one of those old touch tone phones you usually didn't call anybody; you just scared the bejeebies out of the cat.

Later on, when early cell phones came along, you couldn't really butt dial anyone with one of them, either, mostly because you were more likely to carry them around on a flatbed than in a pocket.

The first real chance we had to accidentally dial people came when phones started to get portable enough that we started carrying them around in a pocket

Look, it's a technologically treacherous world we live in today. If you were to accidentally hit "Reply All" to the wrong email, everybody on Traci's Friends List learns that you think Traci's friends are all a bunch of creeps and phonies. Get a little bit curious about how whales breathe, innocently type "blow holes" into a Google search screen and... Well, you can imagine. All I'm saying is, we need to be ever alert and vigilant.

And this brings us around to the real question I think we all have to ask ourselves:

If you carry your smart phone in your jacket pocket, will your car keys call your broker and dump all your Apple stock?

Alpacas I Have Known

Not too long ago I sang and played my guitar at an Alpaca Open House in Indiana. It was at Honey's Alpaca Ranch, not too far from Indianapolis, Indiana, and owned by my cousin Heide and her husband Kurt.

Alpacas make a better audience than you might think. They are not real big on applause, probably because they only have two toes, but at least they don't stand in front of you having shouted conversations with each other while you're playing. And all in all, they seemed to really enjoy the original stuff.

But then I may be taking too much credit. When I first plugged in the guitar microphone and got a blast of feedback, they charged the stage like a herd of fans at a Hanna Montana concert.

I guess calling it an Alpaca Open House was a little misleading, though, since it turns out that the open house was not actually intended for the alpacas – they just happened to live where I was playing. The open house was apparently set up for a bunch of people who had nothing better to do on a Saturday afternoon than drive out to look at alpacas. And maybe hear a little music.

Alpacas really are pretty interesting animals, and I know a lot more about them now than I did a couple of weeks ago. They are kind of like llamas, only they're smaller, they have softer fur, and they have owners who get kind of testy when you call them llamas.

They keep the males and females in separate pens, divided by a fence - which seems like a pretty good idea in general if you stop and think about it. I mean, think how much simpler a man's life would be if all the women were kept on the other side of a good stout partition.

All things considered, life seems to be pretty straightforward for an alpaca. The females basically just wander around all day eating grass, pooping little black pellets, getting their fur sheared off, and occasionally squirting out a baby alpaca. The males spend their days demonstrating to each other what they would be doing if they could just get over to the other side of that good stout partition. I'm not sure I care to know what the guys do at night.

There are a number of things about raising alpacas that are a little bit unusual. For instance, I had an opportunity to go alpaca shopping with Heide and Kurt, who were looking to buy a breeding male.

Understand that I am by no means a farmer, and I had never really given much thought to what we would be looking for in a breeding male alpaca. I supposed they would want nice fur (alpaca ranchers call it "fiber"), or good teeth, or maybe the alpaca equivalent of "bedroom eyes" for getting those girl alpacas in the mood. So I guess I expected the process to go pretty much like you see when somebody buys a horse on television – pat it on the back, stick your fingers in the mouth, gaze into the eyes, and fork over the cash.

What I did not expect was for Kurt to walk right up behind the first prospective alpaca Romeo, who was standing calmly and gazing off into the distance, and grab the little guy by the testicles.

Now I'll admit I don't have a lot of direct experience here, but I would have assumed that just about any male, regardless of species, would prefer to avoid getting grabbed by the testicles. Especially by a stranger.

For those of you who are firing up your laptops to send me angry emails, I am sure there are a few exceptions to that – after all, it takes all kinds. I guess my real point is, you would think that being grabbed by the testicles would get some kind of reaction, one way or another. It is just one of those things that I would find it hard to be neutral about.

But that is exactly how that alpaca treated the situation. He simply gazed over his shoulder as if to say. "Oh, hello there. I'm Doug. Happy to meet you. Will you be buying me then? And if not, would you be so kind as to open the gate over there, the one that leads to the pen where the chicks are?"

Kurt then offered Doug's testicles to Heide, who squeezed them and nodded approvingly. When she offered them to me, I said, "No, thanks anyway. I'm good."

We didn't buy Doug, at least not that day, and after an hour or so I completely lost track of the alpacas we groped. Each time we got the same indifferent response from the gropees, and we ended up leaving, literally if not metaphorically, empty-handed.

Next – I Don't Know Nothing About Birthing No Alpacas!

I Don't Know Nothing About Birthing No Alpacas

Last week I wrote about joining my cousin and her husband on a quest to buy a male alpaca. After discovering that the alpaca equivalent of kicking the tires is to give your prospect's testicles a good squeeze, I have decided that the universal maxim of alpaca shopping should be something like;

No ifs, ands or buts, the proof is in the nuts.

Or,

He'll be a delight if the cojones are right.

Or,

Don't take him back to your shack, if you don't like the sack.

Or... well, I could keep this up pretty much indefinitely, but I think you get the picture. Feel free to come up with your own original ATA (Alpaca Testicle Aphorism) and send it along to me.

He'll make nifty socks if you cuddle his rocks.

The other striking thing that happened during our brief sojourn at the Ranch was the birth of a baby alpaca named Acacia. She was born to a mom whose short, stubby legs earned her a nickname, an affectionate reference to Eddie Murphy's character in *Shrek* - "Donkey."

Now in general, the life of an alpaca does not really shape up to be all that stimulating, even as farm animals go. They pretty much just wander around the barn yard. They occasionally yank a mouthful of grass out of the ground and stand there, chewing slowly and thoughtfully. Since alpacas are not really known to be intellectual giants, I'm guessing that their thoughtfulness is focused on the next mouthful of grass.

So you would think that the birth of a new baby would be a pretty electrifying event around the old alpaca pen. Something that would really break up the monotony.

Not so. While we did not witness the actual moment of birth, we were on the scene within a couple of minutes, and the pasture was almost unnaturally tranquil. My sense is that, at most, Donkey might have been startled into pausing for about one grass munch by the thump of her baby plopping to the earth behind her.

At about three minutes of age Acacia was standing up and trying, with mixed success, to walk. Donkey was standing calmly some distance away, poking at a particularly succulent-looking tuft of grass with her nose.

After we humans shook things up a bit, toweling off the still-wet newborn, weighing her, ooh-ing and ahh-ing and pointing out that her gangly legs were already longer than her mother's, most of the other alpacas began to take notice of the new arrival.

One by one they would come over and give Acacia's head a sort of "welcome to the pen" sniff. Each time, the baby would look up and ask clearly (if you happen to speak alpaca), "Are you my mother?" Of course, she also asked the same question of each of the humans, the resident attack llama, a riding lawn mower, and an ancient Rhodesian Ridgeback dog named Rex.

About the only one she didn't ask was Donkey, who really didn't seem all that interested in the whole situation, one way or the other.

A little while later I held Acacia in my arms for a photo op while she tried to nurse on my ear, and I found myself thinking back to the day my

son was born. After gazing into his oddly familiar face and assuring him that no, I was not his
mother, I spent the rest of the afternoon strutting
around town wearing an "It's A Boy" button and
shoving bubble gum cigars and handfuls of baby
pictures into the hands of everyone who was not
quick-witted enough to outrun me.

How could he be bad if you check out his 'nads?

Sorry. So, anybody want to see some baby
alpaca pictures?

Singing For The Seniors

One by one they came in to find their seats for our concert.

Some of them were leaning on walkers, shuffling carefully along in those little mobile cages, with the two wheels in front and hand brakes. Some of the walkers even had baskets, although I didn't see any with little bells or squeezy horns. In a sense, they were back to depending on a sort of bicycle, like they did as children so many years ago. Only these bikes are (hopefully) a whole lot slower.

A few of them were in powered wheel chairs, gliding silently and triumphantly through the door and down the aisle, driving with their little joysticks and a look of satisfaction. Others were in the old style wheel chairs, this one helped by a uniformed assistant and that one by a younger relative there for a weekend visit.

But many of them were walking with canes or with no assistance at all. It looked like they moved with some pain, though, and they chose each step with care. Some of them bore bruises that were probably the result of making a walking decision that did not entirely pan out.

They were all members of an upscale retirement community, paying to spend an hour on a beautiful springtime Sunday afternoon listening to Kitty Donohoe and I sing some songs and tell some stories about our work with Lost Voices. We were performing in their chapel, a bright, beautiful room with a vaulted ceiling and amazing acoustics. The altar had been moved aside, leaving us a perfect stage.

The first audience member arrived while I was just getting the microphones out of the bags, nearly an hour before the show was scheduled to start. She carefully chose a spot a few seats in from the aisle in the third row and sat patiently, smiling softly and adjusting her hearing aid as I assembled the sound system, tuned the guitars and set all the sound levels. Most of the other seats were full of smiling seniors fifteen minutes early.

We opened the concert with a piece by an outstanding singer/songwriter named Catie Curtis, called "Passing Through." My favorite part of the song is in the last verse:

If I can't change the world,
I'll change the world within my reach.
What better place to start
Than here and now with me and you?
We are only passing through.

As I sang that passage, I looked out at all the faces. Aside from the man in the center of the second row who had dozed off while we were being introduced, every face was rapt, deeply involved. One woman was nodding in time, with tears in her eyes.

Kitty and I spent the rest of our time on stage telling these people all about the group of incarcerated kids who have shared with us brilliant glimpses into their souls. We sang some songs written by those kids, songs about mean streets, and bad decisions, and pain. Songs about relationships they lost, or wished they had. Even songs about the hopes and aspirations and courage of people they would never meet.

All the while our audience tapped their feet and leaned into every word.

As I watched these wonderful people, so gracefully nearing the end of their own long journeys through this world, I found myself deeply moved by the way they were willing to connect emotionally with troubled young men and women whose own roads had gone so wrong so early.

Maybe they saw shadows of their own children, or grandchildren, or even their younger selves in the stories of the Lost Voices kids. Maybe they felt fortunate that those shadows had never fallen across their paths.

And maybe they were just willing to step out of their own challenges for a while, to help us plant a few seeds for some trees under which none of us may ever sit.

A Requiem For Smokers

This afternoon my friend and I dropped into a friendly neighborhood tavern to grab some lunch and to watch the Detroit Red Wings CRUSH the Colorado Avalanche in the second round of the NHL playoffs. Now, if you happen to be a Colorado Avalanche fan, you should know that I deeply respect the Colorado team, and that I also respect you as a fellow sports fan. Cheer up - I'm sure your guys will do better next time out.

Just kidding. The Avs suck.

Anyway, I didn't really want to talk about the hockey game. I want to talk about something else in that tavern, something you can count on finding in lots of bars, along with oceans of alcohol-fueled despair and happy hour hot wing specials. I want to talk about people who smoke cigarettes.

Many years ago, this would not be something that was even worth mentioning. When I was a kid, my parents and the parents of all my friends ate their meals with a fork in one hand and a cigarette in the other. Back then, it seemed like everybody smoked.

And people could smoke just about anywhere they wanted to. Ok, they did discourage smoking in some nursery schools and most operating rooms, and it was considered impolite to actually light up in a crowded elevator, probably because the hair spray on the big-haired lady in front of us was as flammable as napalm. But other than that it was pretty much "smoke 'em if you got 'em."

Old movies probably had a lot to do with this attitude. Many love scenes kicked off with William Powell firing up a Pall Mall and blowing smoke in the face of a (breathless) Myrna Loy. In the sports movies, the home team would get its pep talk from a head coach with a clipboard in one hand and a Camel in the other. In these scenes one or two of the players refrained from smoking, serious athletes that they were - at least until after the game.

I once saw a 1950s Sci-Fi movie in which a rocket crew wearing silver space suits and sitting in oak swivel chairs landed on Mars, turned off their rocket, then sat back and lit up. I can't think of anything quite as refreshing as a nice haze of cigarette smoke when you're living in a pressurized tin can.

Back then, cigarettes were even considered vaguely medicinal. The first thing the plucky corpsman would do after tending to a wounded John Wayne on a stretcher in Iwo Jima would be to shove a lit cigarette in his mouth. Apparently, in World War II-era combat medicine, an effective substitute for antibiotics was emphysema.

These days smokers occupy a rung on the social ladder somewhere between lepers and skunk wranglers. You see them in the designated smoking areas outside office buildings, huddled in hazy little clusters, with their shoulders hunched against the weather and the stark disapproval of society.

About the only other indoor places where you still see people smoking are bars. In fact, in cities like New York and the entire country of Ireland, smoking is prohibited in any public building, bars included. Among other things, this means that in these places all the bars smell a whole lot better – unless, of course, Stinky McOuthouse happens to have passed out under the pool table.

So what has happened?

I think the main thing is that a lot of those really cool people who were almost never seen without a cigarette, people like John Wayne, the Marlboro Man, and, sadly, my parents are – astonishingly - no longer with us. And a lot of us who smoked because we grew up that way have decided to get rid of cigarettes and put off joining them, at least for long enough to get acquainted with our grandchildren.

Besides, it's gotten just plain expensive to smoke. Not only do cigarettes cost about the same as uranium or high grade heroin, a modern smoker can't sell a house or furniture without first fumigating it with, say, napalm. In fact, just having smoked in a car will give it the approximate resale value of a used toilet brush.

So now when I watch someone sitting in a cloud of smoke and putting a cigarette to their lips, it seems kind of strange to me. Anybody care for a mint?

How To Talk Techie

Here in the twenty-first century it is important for a writer to be technologically up-to-date. At a moment's notice we have to be ready to Google, Yahoo, Digg, Backflip, Gather, Bebo, Plaxo, Facebook, Newsvine, Myspace, Fark, Blog, Kaboodle, or Tweet. I have heard rumors that one or two of us actually know what all that stuff means.

Way up toward the top of the modern writer's "You're Pretty Much Screwed If You Don't Have One" list is the Web site. This is an amazing modern communications tool that allows us to present our work to readers in the form of:

"404 ERROR - The Page You Have Requested Is Not Found! It is a safe bet that the doofus who owns this Web site has messed something up, probably forever. Please try again later. Or better yet, give up and go read something else. Like a book."

So I have a Web site. In fact, there is a pretty good chance that if you didn't get a 404 ERROR, you're reading this very column on it.

My Web site is sort of like having a pet. It is generally pretty nice to have around, but it can be a lot of work, and it's really hard to deal with when it gets sick. Sure, a Web site doesn't curl up and sleep on your lap, but it also doesn't leave hair all over the furniture.

Speaking of pets, one night last week my wife said, "I think I messed up my computer. When I tried to go to your Web site I just got a picture of a monkey with a gun."

You should understand that my wife has a sort of love-hate relationship with her computer. She is never happier than when she is on Facebook, taking a quiz to determine which Ewok she is (for you non-nerds, Ewoks are those little furry guys from Star Wars: Return of the Jedi. It turns out, she is Paploo).

On the other hand, she can make smoke come out of the CD-ROM slot by wearing her reading glasses too far down on her nose when she sends an email. Whenever that happens, she finds it upsetting.

Even so, I did not see how she could have done anything that would make a monkey with a gun pop up on her screen, so I decided to check out my Web site. Sure enough, my home page had been replaced by a picture of a chimpanzee pointing a large handgun and wearing a kind of "Che Guevara meets Dirty Harry" expression on his face. Below the picture was a block of text in Portuguese, which in my expert opinion was either something about death to all capitalist warmongers, or a recipe for corn bread.

I immediately called my Web Guru, Todd, to help me clean up the mess. We reinitialized the MX record, cleaned up the config files, reinstalled the CMS, dovetailed all the databases, flipped the bleemis glam (twice), and feather dusted the root.

Actually, I have no idea what we did. I think I may have heard Todd say something about "dovetailing databases," but he might have said, "impaling." Or "baling." "Whaling?"

Basically I followed a whole lot of instructions from Todd in what might as well have been Urdu. Luckily, he seemed to have a pretty good handle on what he was talking about, since we were able to repair everything and get the site back online in a mere 36 hours, not counting Mountain Dew runs, potty stops and breaks for Cool Ranch Doritos.

In our next episode - No, You Didn't Win a Brand New iPhone.

No, You Didn't Win a Brand New iPhone

I love email.

I think email just might be the most powerful communication medium ever invented. Think about it; in a matter of seconds I can fire off a note to a reader in Jakarta, Indonesia thanking her for pointing out that three months ago I stranded a preposition in my column about dog poop. I can let her know that her alert grammatical assistance is something I will always be grateful for.

The best thing about email is that it's all completely free - if you don't count the $49.95 I spend every month on my high speed internet connection, or the roughly $150,000 I have invested in computer equipment that is now worth a total of maybe $75 on a good eBay day.

But there is a downside to all this instant intercontinental kvetching. It's known as SPAM.

For the benefit of my younger readers, the overwhelming majority of whom have grown up roasting their thighs reading email on their laptops, I should point out that back in the old days the word "SPAM" referred to a vaguely meat-like substance that you ate. When I was a kid in Hawaii there was nothing quite as wonderful as a SPAM sandwich, or SPAM and eggs.

On an interesting side note, have you ever heard of a constipated Hawaiian?

Anyway, just imagine my disappointment later in life when the registered trademark of one of my favorite foods became synonymous with email Subject lines like, "You can be ugly and stupid, as long as you have a big tool!" (I'm pretty sure they are not talking about cordless drills).

So what this all boils down to is that each day I get somewhere between fifty and a hundred messages correcting my grammar or providing me with other information vital to my career or my life in general. For each one of these I get at least twenty unsolicited offers to refinance my house or to improve myself in ways that involve enlarging or otherwise enhancing the form and function of certain body parts.

I also get offers to achieve the status I always wanted with a fake Rolex (yeah, but it's a Rolex! Kind of...), watch uncensored Internet TV for free (you can't beat the price, and it's UNCENSORED!), get a Master's Degree without attending any classes (I'm thinking that just might be where Sarah Palin's strategists went to school), earn hundreds a day working out of my home (hundreds of what?), buy software for all needs and budgets (with all the documentation dated 1996 and written in Mandarin), or discover the "Blueberry path to better sex in America(?!?)."

I particularly enjoy the note I get about once a month from the widow of a Nigerian diplomat who perished in an unfortunate automobile accident, leaving $25 million in an offshore bank account. The Widow has utmost faith in my righteousness and reliable nature, and she is sure that God wants her to give me all that money so I can make good use of it. The note is always addressed to "fartengood@learnedsofar.com" and begins, "My Dearest Friend Fartengood."

Then there are the "giveaways." Call me a cynic, but I am willing to bet that not a lot of people have ever actually received a brand-new iPhone in return for filling out a "brief online survey." Oh sure, these things look perfectly legitimate, asking for your Social Security number and a major credit card just to make sure you're over eighteen and eligible to operate an iPhone. Still, I have my doubts.

So what can we do about all this SPAM? If we can't stop it, can we at least control how many SPAM messages make it to our In Box? Does the bandwidth wasted by SPAM threaten the future of the Web and our entire civilization? Do "beautiful horny housewives right in my town" really want to get to know me better? Am I getting tired of all these stupid semi-rhetorical questions?

Next up - Go Out and Hug a Hacker

Go Out and Hug a Hacker

A couple of weeks ago I mentioned that someone had replaced my home page with a picture of a monkey holding a gun, despite all sorts of server and network security. I have passwords for my passwords, and more passwords that allow me to get to the other passwords. And still they defeated all those levels of security and got in.

And what they did once they got in was post a picture of a monkey holding a gun.

The obvious question is, "Why would anyone want to replace my home page with a picture of a monkey holding a gun?"

People who do things like this are called "hackers." They can be easily identified among the people you know if they display one or more of the following signs:

1. A computer with at least three monitors.

2. A computer with a water-cooled CPU.

3. A diploma from MIT hanging next to a Led Zeppelin poster.

4. Carpal tunnel syndrome in both wrists.

5. A half-inch crust of Doritos crumbs coating the belly of a Led Zeppelin t-shirt.

6. A Dell laptop running "Ubuntu Linux."

7. The remotest idea what "Ubuntu Linux" might be.

Nobody is entirely sure exactly where this connotation of the term "hacker" comes from. The word "hack" derives from the Old English word "tohaccian," which long ago meant "To chop something into pieces and let the remains scatter over the belly of your Ledde Zepplinne hauberk."

The term apparently first showed up in the early 1960s among a group of computer-addicted undergrads at - you guessed it - MIT. They called themselves the "Tech Model Railroad Club," presumably hoping that they might someday line themselves up a little "Caboose."

Hackers seem to take pride in attacking and solving difficult technical puzzles in innovative ways. A good hacker will spend weeks writing code that can sniff a password, then break into and crawl a Web server to locate the owner's email address. Then they can send him an email that says, "Blisters." This approach is a lot more elegant than clicking the "Contact Us" link in the menu on the home page.

Sometimes hackers are simply playing practical jokes, following a rich and storied tradition of binary code-based wit and humor. According to an authoritative (as far as I know) hacker Web site called "The Jargon File", a prime example of this hilarity popped up in 2001 when programmers in Bergen, Norway "pinged" each other by logging messages sent by - get this - carrier pigeons!

Here is the punchline from the classic log they generated on that historic day:

-- 10.0.3.1 ping statistics --

9 packets transmitted, 4 packets received, 55% packet loss

round-trip min/avg/max = 3211900.8/5222806.6/6388671.9 ms

vegard@gyversalen:~$ exit

Can you believe those packet times? Man, the laughs just keep on coming!

Some hackers are not all that harmless. They can cause serious malicious damage to whole networks, steal credit card information, compromise national security, and commit all sorts of other crimes. In fact, over the years a whole new field of law enforcement has grown up, designed to catch these evil hackers with the help of other hackers, many of whom have been rendered considerably less evil by spending a couple of years in a cell with no broadband connection. Or Doritos.

The bottom line is, without hackers the computer world would be a far less interesting place. For one thing, we would never have developed the kind of razor-sharp computer security protocols we enjoy in Microsoft Windows Vista, the cutting-edge operating system that responds to a maintenance update on your copy of Microsoft Word by canceling your American Express card and erasing your hard drive.

So I suggest that we all make an effort now and then to appreciate hackers, those brilliant people who have way too much time on their hands. And, who could probably really use a hug.

Ask Dr. Mike - Relationships, Transmissions, and a High-Pitched "Yee, Hee"

Dr. Mike is an advice columnist whose main qualification for dispensing life-changing wisdom is his Ph.D. in Soap Opera Appreciation from the University of Tim Online (all major credit cards accepted).

Here is what fell out of this week's mail bag:

Dear Dr. Mike,

I don't know what to do about my marriage. My husband came home last night and seemed very pre-occupied. When I tried to cheer him up by suggesting that we go out to dinner at his favorite restaurant, Casey's, he just shrugged and grabbed the car keys.

He barely spoke through dinner, and when I asked him what was wrong, he just said, "Nothing." He had a beer before dinner, and another one after

the meal arrived. On the way home I tried every-
thing I could think of to cheer him up, but it was as
if he was on another planet. If he answered me at all,
it was only to grunt, "yes" or, "no."

When we got home, he just opened another beer
and sat down to watch the hockey game. I went to
bed alone and cried myself to sleep.

Dr. Mike, I'm worried. It's as if he doesn't even
know I'm alive any more. I read an article in a wom-
en's magazine not too long ago, all about sure signs
that you've lost your man. It could have been written
about us last night. The only thing he hasn't done yet
is buy me a box of "guilt chocolates."

So what do I do? Is my husband in love with
someone else? Have I lost him forever?

Signed with my tears,

My Life Is Over in Ann Arbor

Dear Over,

Beats me. Somebody sent me a copy of that
article you're talking about, and it does seem like
beer and grunting might have been mentioned in
there somewhere. Bummer.

So anyway, have a great day!

Dear Dr. Mike,

I'm kind of worried. Driving home yesterday
the truck started making a high-pitched whine that
sounded like it might be coming from the differential.

On the up-side, I found out that Casey's has my favorite beer on tap, and the Wings won.

So what do you think, am I going to be on the hook for a new transmission?

I'd Rather Buy A Boat in Ann Arbor

Dear Rather,

Maybe, although I'm thinking that it might just be a torque converter or something as simple as the pressure control solenoid valve. Also, and this is just a hunch, you might want to avoid buying your wife any chocolates.

Dear Dr. Mike,

I came home the other night and found my teenage son and some of his friends playing a Michael Jackson dance game on the Wii. I was amazed to see my son, who has always hated to dance, executing perfect moonwalks and crotch grabs in front of an animated King of Pop and a group of animated support dancers. I had to admit, my son was pretty good at it.

So, should I be concerned?

Signed,

I Liked Michael Better Back When He Was A Black Kid

Dear Liked,

I wouldn't worry too much. This is just a video game, and dancing is good exercise. All in all, it might be considered a good thing for your son. Unless, of course, he starts setting up sleepovers with Cub Scout troops.

So that's it for another Dr. Mike. If you would like to get advice on your most important personal problems from a guy who writes jokes for a living, just send an email to Mike@learnedsofar.com. The odds are pretty good that he won't completely destroy your life.

Starting Out

My son is going to get married in a little less than a month. For my wife and I this is the coolest thing ever, since we are crazy about his fiance, her parents, her brother, her friends - and her taste in guys. As the weeks go by, all the wedding plans are proceeding more or less normally for the kids, with nervousness over all the details spiraling steadily up past anxiety and into flat-out hysteria.

All this elaborate wedding-planning stuff is a little bit foreign to Nan and me. Thirty-four years ago when we got married, we had a quick service in a tiny stone church (she wore a peasant dress, and I splurged for a sport coat) followed by a really fun potluck at a friend's house. With a pool.

Yes, the groom did go swimming with all the other kids.

Not that I am complaining. Shannon and Patrick have some terrific ideas for their wedding, and whether or not everything goes exactly as they have planned it, the day will be as beautifully unique as it will be wonderful. I wish I had even the slightest chance of convincing them to just relax, that no matter how the day turns out, it will be perfect.

As we hurdle toward the great occasion, I find myself spending a lot of time thinking about how happy I am for them. But not as much for the wedding itself as for the new family that is about to be born. They have invested in a house of their own, complete with a mortgage, worn-out siding, a fifty pound box of nails, enough paint to float the Queen Mary, and a seemingly bottomless charge account at Home Depot - everything they need to make that house a home.

In other words, the kids are doing what is known as "just starting out," and I really envy them. This is one case where the story really is a lot more about the journey than about the destination.

And what a journey they have to look forward to. They will get to worry about car payments and dandelions. They will get to scrape meals together out of whatever is left in the fridge from the weekend. They will get to take turns trying to figure out the income taxes. With a little luck, they will get to take turns trying to figure out how to deal with a kid or two.

They are embarking on a life-long power struggle over the TV remote.

So kids, get out there and have fun with all the giggles and tears you're signing up for. And enjoy the adventure. You might think that it would be convenient to know up front how it's all going to turn out, but where's the fun in that?

The funny thing is, whenever I look at Shannon and Patrick and their new life, all I can think about is how much it feels like Nan and I are still just starting out ourselves. OK, so we've logged a lot of miles, and we've put a scratch or two on the fenders; the road has been pretty rough sometimes.

But I can swear that there are still times - like when I'm trying to work out how I'm going to get a rewrite done on deadline, or pay for a new water softener - that I find myself looking over at her. And in those moments I can always still detect just a hint of that new-car smell.

One Last Job For the Big Day

The kids will be getting married in less than a week now. I find myself walking around with a big stupid grin on my face at the thought that my son - who I am pretty sure does not yet know how to tie his own necktie - will be standing up before God and all his pals (my son's pals, not necessarily God's) to promise the rest of his life to his new bride. I am completely certain that Shannon and Pat will be the best bride and groom ever.

They live about two hours away from us, so I can only assume that all the preparations are going well. At least, we haven't received any hysterical phone calls. We did see this message posted to Shannon's Facebook page:

Things I need ASAP:

A.) Someone to drive an 18 passenger old school Dodge shuttle van from the hotel to the wedding site (approx 3 miles) from 4:30-5:30 & 10:30-11:30pm.

I can pay you, you just need to be sober.

B) A bagpiper that doesn't cost an arm and a leg from 5pm-6pm.

oh yeah... AND I need 3 strong boys that wanna help Pat get two 300 lb. cement flower pots out of his truck tonight at the wedding site. They are VERY heavy!

I thought about picking up the phone to tell her that as a general rule you are better off if you don't cut corners when it comes to your bagpipers.

I could see in an instant, though, just why Pat had picked this amazing young woman to be his wife. There is a really charming practicality in listing sobriety as a stated prerequisite for the shuttle driver, and making certain that everyone was perfectly clear on the idea that those 300lb cement flower pots are VERY heavy.

One thing Shannon asked me to do for the wedding was to dig out and scan a bunch of snapshots of Pat growing up, so she could use them in a slide presentation. This was the best assignment ever, since I got to spend hours wading through pictures of my six-year old son running through Disney World with elastic-waisted shorts showcasing his knobby knees, and a Steamboat

Willie sailor's hat pushing his ears out like little pink airplane wings.

There were shots of him in full-out snorkeling gear exploring a swimming pool in Florida while his mom and his grandparents sat in the shade talking about how Alice from the old hometown had a bad case of shingles. There were team pictures from ten years of youth ice hockey, showing my young warrior growing progressively taller and more mature in each frame, always leaning on a hockey stick and trying to look fierce for the camera.

There were pictures of him practicing wakeboard tricks on the trampoline, then exploding into the water trying those tricks out behind the boat. There were shots of him dressing up Brenna the Dog in a Conquistador helmet, to the obvious (believe it or not) delight of Brenna the Dog.

There were pictures of him smiling through a chin caked with strained carrots, of him trying to tame a wild rocking horse, of him laughing hysterically at Mommy in a scooter cap.

On Saturday the kids will be starting out on their own journey. With a little luck they will spend more years together than they can imagine right now, building their new branch of the family and working their way through a wonderful maze of fun and fears and triumphs.

Along the way maybe they will fill up a picture drawer or two of their own.

And Now They Are One

Well, they pulled it off. My son and my new daughter (that "in-law" stuff seems like a pretty impersonal way to talk about the love of my child's life) have joined hands and become husband and wife. And I'm here to tell you that their wedding was absolutely, positively the most beautiful event in the history of the world.

The plan was really amazing. The whole thing was held outdoors on the grounds surrounding the country home of their friend, Timmy. There was a "chapel" set up with bales of hay making up the pews and an arch beautifully decorated to form the altar. On the other side of the house there was a giant tent, decorated as elegantly as any banquet hall, to house the reception. There were neat signs, hand-painted on driftwood, and other clever details everywhere, all perfectly designed to make the wedding uniquely theirs.

OK, if you want to be technical about it, I'll admit that there were a few unexpected hitches in the celebration. Some elements did not come off exactly as planned. There were a few bumps in the road, a little sand in the peanut butter. Or to put it bluntly, just about everything that could go wrong, did go wrong.

To hit just a few highlights, the wedding day turned out to be one of the coldest October days in the history of Grand Rapids, Michigan. Still, we were all thankful that at least the sun was shining - until about an hour before the ceremony, when a bank of clouds black enough to intimidate the Wicked Witch of the West rolled in. We were looking up at those clouds and congratulating ourselves that at least it was not raining, when it began to drizzle.

Then, just as we were getting ready to start the ceremony, I heard someone nearby say, "Well at least it's not raining all that hard!" A moment later, the wind kicked up to gale force and the rain turned into sleet. And after that... well, I think you get the picture.

But as I sat there on my bale of hay in the front row of the wedding ceremony, sleet mingling with my tears of absolute happiness, I realized that I was as proud of those two kids as it is possible to be. It was clear that my son and my New Daughter had found their way past the little dents and dings in their party plans and made it to that special place reserved for lovers and other lunatics. They were looking into each other's eyes and grinning, safe and warm in a glowing bubble of joy that kept all the imperfections of the world around them at bay.

And later, as they danced under the tent and hugged each other and their friends; as Shannon, wearing a sweatshirt to cover her bare shoulders, grinned and showed off the tar-black halo of mud on the hem of her wedding dress; as Pat made sure everyone saw the cowboy boots he was wearing with his tuxedo; as Kid Rock's voice sang "... sweet home Alabama, all summer long!" through the PA speakers while frost formed on the speaker poles, that glow was not only still there, it was shining more brightly each time one of them caught the other's eye.

So to be completely accurate, I guess I would have to say that the wedding was not perfect. It was way, way, WAY better than that!

Thanksgiving On the Brink

"Of course we'll have Thanksgiving at our house this year, Aunt Ellen! I'll write notes to everyone and tell them!" Mom hung up the phone with a crooked smile and began to sing softly to herself;

Oh where did I leave that bottle of Scotch
The bottle of Scotch, my sweet bottle of Scotch?
Oh where did I leave that bottle of Scotch?
It's half past nine in the morning...

Great Aunt Ellen had just explained that for the first time in a generation she and Great Uncle Charlie could not host the family's annual Thanksgiving get-together. It seems that over the weekend Great Uncle Charlie tried to repair a drain in the kitchen sink, and the federal hazmat teams will not be finished with the house until mid-January.

This news did not make Mom all that happy. The last time she was in charge of hosting a family get-together was the Christmas best remembered for the Canine Culinary Calamity, in which the humans dined on canned corned beef from the Speedway while Carl the Dog and Bernie The Schnauzer feasted on the spiral-sliced ham that was forgotten at the bottom of Grandma and Grandpa's garbage bag of gifts.

"Must prepare. Need help. Everyone coming here in a week. No time. Oh God. No time."

"Mom," shouted Todd Junior from the up-stairs bathroom, "Do we have more bath towels?"

"Why Dear?"

"Because there are only nine in here, and it doesn't look like that's going to be enough to soak up all the toilet water on the floor."

An hour later the Family was assembled in the living room for a Council of War.

"OK, here's the story," said Mom, pacing Patton-like back and forth in front of her troops, "I'll need cooperation from all of you so we can get this place ready for company."

"OK Mom," said Little Suzie, her thumbs flying over the keyboard of her cell phone as she typed a text message to her friend Heather; OMG, my mom is so lame. LOL!

"Sure thing Honey," said Dad, his thumbs flying over the keyboard of his cell phone as he tried to find a way to turn it on. "I'll get right on that."

"Hey, what's this stuff?" said Todd Junior, dumping the contents of the decorative oil lamp in the carpet. "Anybody got a match?"

As the week wore on the Family pitched in. Mom vacuumed and dusted every corner of the house, washed the windows, dry cleaned the drapes, waxed the kitchen floor, shampooed the lamp oil out of the living room carpet, repainted the guest room, changed the shelf paper in the pantry, rewired the furnace, and replaced all the warped floor tiles in the upstairs bathroom.

Little Suzie dusted and organized her Barbie's Beach House, cleaned up the pantry, and helped Mom with the electrical work.

Todd Junior added a mural to the freshly-painted guest room wall, a sort of abstract rendition of Original Sin and Exile from the Garden, executed in red Rustoleum left over from repainting the Swing Set, and purple Magic Marker.

Dad purchased a fifteen-foot tall inflatable turkey and installed it in the front yard.

And then came Thanksgiving day. Aunt Karen and Uncle Fred brought Cousins Sheldon and Brittany, five pounds of oyster stuffing, and a pecan pie. Aunt Meg and Uncle Bob brought cousins Pammie and the Twins, five pounds of canned yams, and a pumpkin pie. Great Aunt Ellen and Uncle Charlie brought Carl the Dog, five pounds of 3-bean salad, and a cherry cheesecake. Uncle Stan and Aunt Stacey brought Baby Sam, five pounds of mashed potatoes and a mincemeat pie. Grandma and Grandpa brought a box of extra sweaters for Grandpa, five pounds of Metamucil, and a package of Urinal Cakes.

Overall, the day went well, other than Grandpa cranking the thermostat up to the "Surface of the Sun" setting and blowing out the new furnace wiring. And Todd Junior, Sheldon and the twins hiding all the furniture from Barbie's Malibu Mansion in the bowl of yams. And the horrifying but surprising fragrant aftermath of Bernie the Schnauzer and Carl the Dog getting into that box of Urinal Cakes.

But the turkey was great, there was plenty of other food to make up for those yams, and more than enough love to go around.

Happy Thanksgiving, everybody!

Santwilight

OK, has anybody besides me noticed that Santa Claus is not getting as much attention as he used to get? At Christmas time when I was a kid, you could not throw a candy cane without hitting a fat guy in a red suit and beard. It seemed like every TV, magazine or newspaper ad featured the old boy peeking out from behind a Christmas tree, or holding up a bottle of Coke with a carbo-hydrate-fueled twinkle in his eye.

What happened? These days all we see are strangely-dressed pre-teen girls doing drum-line dance routines, mannequins sliding across the ice in Rockefeller Plaza, and Geoffrey the Giraffe helping some little animated children loot a Toys R Us store. Santa has been all but forgotten.

Well, I've decided to do something about this situation. First, I came to the conclusion that here in the Information Age everybody should know just a little bit more about Santa. It seems logical that if people understand him better, they might like him more.

So I got busy and went to work on the problem with my new BFFs Angela and Jessica, blew off the surfing party on the Indian Reservation, dug around in some books of old Quileute legends, and came to a startling conclusion:

Santa Claus is a vampire!

I mean, think about it. He's like, what, eighteen hundred years old? We know that he is really fast, because he can get to houses all around the world in one night. He must be pretty strong, because he hauls around a bag full of presents for nearly seven billion people. And did you ever see Santa hook up with anybody who wasn't just a tad on the cute-but-angst-ridden-outcast side?

I didn't think so.

Now I'm guessing that Santa has always felt like he had to disguise his true nature and hide the whole vampire thing. And to be fair, that made sense. I can see people getting a little bit uptight over a blood-sucking abomination of nature, even a jolly one, breaking in through the chimney and wandering around the house.

In other words, it's like for all these years the whole "bringing presents" and "sainthood" routines were just Santa's heartfelt attempt to fit in.

But these days things have changed. Being a vampire might actually help Santa's image - especially among kids like those drum-line dancers in the Gap ad. We have always loved a bad boy, especially one who is not really all that bad. Maybe the time has come for Santa to let it all hang out.

Santa, here's what I suggest you do. To start with, why not drop a few pounds? Back in the day, fat and jolly was all the rage, but now you really come off more as a walking heart attack. Are those red cheeks a manifestation of holiday cheer, or essential hypertension?

Also, lose the beard. It's just not relevant any more. You should leave some sideburns and shave them to a point, which will also serve to visually thin your face out a little bit. A little chin stubble is fine. You can either stay with the white hair, which might get a kind of Richard Gere thing going for you, or go ahead and dye it - your call on this one.

That red suit definitely has to go. Not only do the fur collar and cuffs mess you up with PETA, you really should be doing black denim. It's hip, sexy - and slimming.

And as for the sleigh, I understand the need for cargo capacity, but a motorcycle has a LOT more Mojo. I'm just saying.

So Santa, come on out of the coffin. Let us see the real you at last. If you follow my suggestions, I think you can get right back to being the most popular person of all time.

Unless, of course, the Easter Bunny turns out to really be a werewolf - then you could have a fight on your hands.

Christmas Songs

Silent night. Holy night.

Only since we're singing, it's not really all that silent, is it? Aren't we actually making all sorts of racket about this alleged "Silent Night" instead of enjoying the silence of it? Could this be the reason we find our world in a never-ending spiral of moral decline? Or of Jingle Bells? I start asking myself questions like these every year, the first time I walk into a Mall and hear the soulful strains of "Grandma Got Run Over By A Reindeer."

Face it, Americans are Christmas Song junkies. For some reason we never seem to get our fill of Bing Crosby's lust for snow, Nat King Cole's chestnut fetish, or Gene Autry's tale of a bunch of reindeer bullying a colleague with rhynophymia (a pathologically red nose). A person who will fire off an angry email to a radio station if they play the same Feist song twice in a fiscal quarter will happily listen to the Chipmunks sing about Alvin's hula hoop every fifteen minutes, all day, every day from Thanksgiving to Christmas.

And I'll admit it, I am that person. I'm a total Christmas Music Junkie.

First off, I find a lot of the Christmas songs really touching. When I was about eight years old I nearly cried when I heard "The Little Drummer Boy" for the first time. I could see myself as the poor child who found himself in the presence of the newborn King of Kings with nothing to give but his simple musical gift. And that song has affected me pretty much the same way every one of the 745,987, 212 times I've heard it since.

Although, have you ever stopped to wonder why any mother, even the infinitely loving and tolerant Blessed Virgin, would be crazy enough to let a kid with a drum into a nursery filled with livestock? Do you have any idea how bad just one rim shot could spook a cow?

A really cool aspect of Christmas music is the fact that every songwriter seems at some point in their career to get hopped up on candy canes and write a Christmas piece or two. And pretty much every singer who ever chipped a tooth on a microphone does entire Christmas shows or has cranked out at least one album of Christmas songs.

Maybe I should make that "Holiday" songs,

since one of my all-time favorites is Adam Sandler's "Chanukah Song;"

> *Put on your yarmulke*
> *Here comes Chanukah*
> *So much funikah*
> *To celebrate Chanukah*
> *Chanukah is the festival of lights*
> *Instead of one day of presents*
> *We get eight crazy nights...*

This season I had the privilege of playing a Holiday Concert with my friend Peter Madcat Ruth, who lives here in the Ann Arbor area and happens to be one of the finest harmonica players in the world. We did a bunch of standards, and I got to demonstrate how an Irish guy sings in Spanish, with "Feliz Navidad" and "Donde Esta Santa Claus." I especially liked our instrumental medley of "The Holly & The Ivy," "Good King Wencislaus," and some other great tunes, in which I got to put away the guitar and lay down a Celtic drum rhythm on my McDjembe.

And it turns out that I'm no exception to the "musician hopped up on candy canes" rule. I've written two Christmas songs that I always haul out this time of year. One is called "A Perfect Day;"

> *At six AM on Christmas day*
> *The children come alive*

Some assembly was required
Dad got to sleep at half past five...

The other is "Carlson the Pissed Off Angel," a parable about a guardian angel who really doesn't care all that much for his client;

My name is Carlson - I'm an angel.
But I can't hang out in Heaven; I have to work.
I've been assigned to take care of a guy named Bob
And he's a jerk...

Don't feel too sorry for Carlson, though. He discovers in the end that the Boss really does know what he's doing.

So for all of you who love the music of this crazy wonderful season like I do, I hope you'll be home to deck the halls, and ring the jingle bells, and have yourself a merry little holly, jolly Christmas – if only in your dreams.

Mirth and Wisdom Teeth

I discovered a new way to observe the Holidays this year; I had a couple of wisdom teeth merrily yanked out of my head. This decision admittedly had less to do with celebrating the end of another year and honoring cultural traditions than it did with using up the last of my dental insurance, but there it is.

Dentists have been trying to get me to have this done since I was in my twenties, but I've stood fast. Among other things, I was reluctant to lose the only things in my life to which you could properly apply the word "wisdom." In fact, it seems like having wisdom teeth extracted is something most guys try to avoid or postpone as a matter of principle - kind of like rectal exams and sorting laundry.

But finally this year, when my dentist made yet another plea for maxillary sanity and the stars moved into the proper alignment with my policy benefits, I realized that the time had come at last. Plus, it dawned on me that if I played my cards right, I could be in for a pretty good nitrous oxide buzz.

My oral surgeon is a very nice man, calm and personable. His voice has a quality that you might even call reassuring. During my initial examination, he cracked jokes and patiently informed me of all the possible medical outcomes. He said that the procedure might be fairly easy, or that it might take "a little more effort."

Later, the friendly and highly professional young woman at the front desk shared some insight into that whole concept of "a little more effort," explaining that as the difficulty of the extraction increased, so would the cost - and my copay. I thought, "Well hey, let's go ahead with it anyway. I'm a lucky guy. Plus, I'm having surgery during the holiday season - what could possibly go wrong?"

Finally the big day arrived. I sat in the chair waiting for the local anesthetic to take effect and listening to a soothing selection of new-age music, confident in the knowledge that I was just imagining the shrieks of agony and maniacal laughter coming from the other treatment rooms.

Later, as I slipped into the gentle haze of the laughing gas, I could see and hear everything going on around me. This amazing stuff has the effect of leaving you awake, but making you pretty much indifferent to whatever is going on. At that moment you could have got me to sort laundry.

Even so, I felt a slight apprehension when the surgeon jammed a chunk of rubber in my mouth and said, "Here, this will give you a little something to bite down on." Then the nitrous kicked back in, and I felt almost relaxed when he said, "OK, now you might hear just a little bit of crunching."

Until that exact moment, I thought I was pretty familiar with the meaning of the word "understatement." As it turns out, I was not even close.

What I heard was more like crushing a block of granite with a gigantic nutcracker. If I had not been biting down on a chunk of rubber, I probably would have asked why every time I heard "a little bit of crunching," I could feel the shock wave in my knees.

But there was my oral surgeon's reassuring voice, periodically checking to see how I was doing and explaining to his assistant that some ethnic groups tended to have very long thin roots, and that, believe it or not, their teeth were even more difficult to work with than mine. After about eight or nine hundred hours of this, I heard those welcome words;

"Are you alive? We're halfway done."

It turns out I was in fact alive, so I gave what I considered a spunky "thumbs up."

At that point, and for the final nine hundred hours, I kind of went out-of-body, my consciousness splitting in two. One part of me totally embraced the nitrous, listening with some amusement to the conversation in the room and trying to come up with rhymes for "searing pain." Fearing rain? Peering at Jane? Cheering the train?

The other, oddly lucid part of me kind of peeked up out of the anesthetic, calculated that we were well into "a little more effort" territory, and started adding up all my liquid assets, trying to come up with what I could sell to cover that rapidly increasing copay.

At long last it was over. I spent the next few days with my jaw puffed up like Angelina Jolie's lips and making sure I didn't try to eat anything crunchier than mashed potatoes. The oral surgeon's office called to make sure I was still alive, to see if I had any further questions or problems, and to give me the heartwarming news that my check had cleared.

And so, it looks like 2011 is going to be a great new year - at least as long as the Tylenol with codeine holds out.

It's Christmas Eve!
Is This Your Chafing Dish?

The Dodge pulls into the driveway at Grandma's House. Mom, Dad, Todd Junior and little Susie are all quivering with anticipation and full bladders as they limp up the driveway, trying to stamp a little blood flow back into legs and feet made all tingly and numb by Dad's unwillingness to pull off the highway while so much as a pint of gas remains in the tank.

Grandma's front door swings open and the succulent Christmas aromas of roast turkey and mince meat pie dance in the crisp December air, laced with just a hint of Vicks VapoRub and moth crystals, and hotter than an afternoon in Death Valley.

Louise, Grandma and all the other women raise the traditional Banshee Wail of Greetings and Hugs, while Aunt Bertha gives the children wet garlicky kisses and pinches them on their Dodge-weary little behinds. Dad goes into pack-mule-mode from car to house, balancing boxes full of gifts, scalloped potatoes, child-rearing equipment, and unfamiliar serving dishes that turned up in the booty from the last reunion.

Within minutes Dad is in the garage with the other men, standing next to a sputtering turkey fryer with a beer in his hand. Mom has joined other women in the kitchen, conspiring on the perfect recipe for Candied Yams. Todd Junior is engaged in a fist fight with Carla's Tommie over who would win in a cage match SmackDown, Barack Obama or God. Charlene's oldest boy, Randy, has let the cat into the spare bedroom where the parakeet flies free, providing an unex-pected holiday feast for little Puffylumpkins. Little Susie and Carla's twins are in the parlor playing European Union Financial Crisis Barbie.

After slightly less time than it took for the glaciers to make their way across North America, dinner is ready. Charlene's middle boy, Luke, somehow sat in the Candied Yams, so he's in the bathroom putting on a pair of Grandpa's old ber-muda shorts. Charlene is back in the kitchen fluff-ing up the Candied Yams. All the other children are seated around card tables set up in the middle of a large tarp in the living room, trading volleys of creamed carrots and mashed potatoes while

Charlene's other middle boy, Thor, sobs, "I-hi-hi wa-hant fre-he-he-hench fries."

The adults sit around the dining room table listening to Aunt Doris' detailed recounting of deceased relatives dating back to the builders of Stonehenge, while the one lone housefly left over from last summer decides to end it all in the gravy boat. Uncle Edgar sleeps leaning back in his chair, snoring through a mouthful of clam dressing. Mom and Charlene head for the living room to determine if Charlene's youngest, Beelzebub, will need stitches. Grandma and Grandpa have one of their typical conversations;

Grandma: "I wish now and then you'd eat some peas."

Grandpa: "Whaddya mean the fish has fleas? That's dumb."

Grandma: "Who broke their thumb?"

After dinner, it's Gift Time! Everyone opens each package with unbridled excitement; "Wow! Tater Mitts! How did you know?"

Finally, post-gravy gravity and televised football overcome the men, so they scatter, Budweiser in hand, onto every available piece of furniture in the living room. The women are in the kitchen, scraping turkey crust off pans, loading the dishwasher, and drinking white zinfandel out of a box.

As the football game gives way to an interview with a player thanking Jesus for causing the other team to fumble at the five yard line, the men begin to regain consciousness. Turkey scraps wind up in sandwiches on reheated dinner rolls, and the last of the pie is consumed over protests of, "...just a sliver... oh my, that's huge, I couldn't possibly... well ok, after all, it's Christmas."

Finally, it's dark outside and everyone gathers up leftovers, child-rearing equipment and any identifiable remains of gifts. The women raise the Banshee Wail Of Departure and Hugs, while the men pack boxes, bags and inert children into the cars. Each family is expected to take home at least one unfamiliar serving dish and leave at least one glove, mitten or child behind. And as the taillights disappear into the night, each family heading for home, Grandpa is heard to say,

"Rome? Who's going to Rome? Damn-it, nobody ever tells me anything..."

2010 - The Year in Preview

OK, we've got 2009 behind us. Once again it's time for me to dust off the Ouija Board, lay out the Tarot Cards, gaze at the coffee grounds (I'm not too crazy about tea), get into the old Rum & Eggnog, and let you all in on what's going to happen in the coming year.

January: The University of Michigan football team fails to play in a bowl game for the second year in a row, after 33 straight postseason appearances. Dedicated U of M fans take up a collection to buy second-year head coach Rich Rodriguez a one-way bus ticket to West Virginia. Dedicated West Virginia University fans chip in and buy him a ticket back to Ann Arbor.

February: The 2010 Winter Olympic Games kick off in Vancouver, British Columbia. American bloggers immediately begin to criticize Michael Phelps for not winning a single gold medal.

Phelps replies, "I'm sorry for letting you all down. The only excuse I have is that all of my events are in the Summer Olympics."

March: Dick Cheney accuses President Obama of time-traveling to 2006 and shooting GOP contributor Harry Whittington in the face while quail hunting. Cheney says that "This fits the overall pattern of this Administration's refusal to keep America safe, or even to admit that we are at war with small, fat, nearly-flightless birds."

The official response from the White House is, "Wait, what?"

April: The first robin of spring is spotted in West Park in Ann Arbor, Michigan, asking picnickers if they have any spare change.

On Tax Day a couple hundred angry Tea Partiers stage an anti-tax rally in Washington, D.C. When a passing certified public accountant points out that their taxes have actually been reduced significantly since President Obama took office, they beat him senseless with hand-lettered signs reading, "Be Smortt - Opose Tyraney" and, "Wize Up, Moran."

May: Golf superstar Tiger Woods gives his wife, Elin Nordegren, a diamond-encrusted solid gold "Cupid's Arrow" as a combination reconciliation and Mother's Day gift. Later in the day Woods is spotted walking bow-legged out of a

Florida emergency room after undergoing "surgical extraction of a diamond-encrusted object" from an unspecified part of his anatomy.

June: The Detroit Tigers are having a rough season after losing Curtis Granderson, Fernando Rodney, Placido Polanco, and several other key players. Dedicated fans take up a collection to buy the entire team bus tickets to West Virginia.

July: On the 4th of July, Americans set an all-time record for the one-day consumption of brats, baked beans and potato salad. On the 5th of July the EPA announces a new alternative energy strategy, harvesting the cloud of methane hovering over the Midwestern United States.

August: Nothing at all happens, since everyone is on vacation.

September: The big new "Back To School" fad item for kids this year is the iWii, a pocket-sized online gaming system that lets kids sit on the playground participating in healthy games like "Virtual Dodge Ball" and "eTag."

October: The Detroit Tigers win the World Series! On a related note, pigs are spotted flying over Ypsilanti and there is an ice hockey tournament in Hell (that's Hell, Hell - not Hell, Michigan).

November: In the last few days before the 2010 Mid-term Elections, the Republican National Committee takes up a collection to buy bus tickets to West Virginia for all the Democrats. West Virginia finally gives up and hops on a bus to North Carolina.

December: Former Alaska Governor Sarah Palin fires a hunting rifle at a Christmas Eve intruder in her home. She describes the intruder as "... a fat hippie in a red suit." Luckily for all of us, Mrs. Palin was shooting from the hip and missed.

Well, those are my predictions and I'm sticking to them. Just bear in mind that if any of these things actually happen, it will all be news to me.

Happy New Year, everybody!

Lost Voices – I Feel Like an Angel With a Broken Wing

This past week my friend Kitty Donohoe and I wrapped up an eight week Lost Voices program at an alternative high school for kids who have not been able, for one reason or another, to thrive in normal high schools. Five days later, I'm still trying to catch my breath.

I think by now that a lot of you have at least heard of Lost Voices, for the simple reason that I never stop babbling about it. But it seems that most people simply know that we work with troubled kids, and have no idea what actually goes on.

Well, here's your chance to find out.

This last program was a little different for us than the ones we've done in the past, for two reasons. First, the kids in this group are not incarcerated. Now, as a performer I have always done better with audiences who have abandoned all hope of escape, so this did present quite a challenge for me.

The bigger issue, though, is that at the end of the day incarcerated kids are locked up in their rooms with their thoughts and their journals, while many of the young people who attend this alternative school finish each day by returning to the environments that had at least something to do with getting them into trouble in the first place.

This means that each day when they get back to school most of them have to scale, to at least some extent, the same mountains they had to conquer the day before. At this particular school, the kids were in an atmosphere nurtured by an incredibly talented and motivated faculty and staff to help them climb.

The second difference is that this was the first co-ed group we've dealt with.

Now, I've done a lot of work with teenagers over the years, including coaching a high school boys hockey team, which was kind of like paddling a canoe through a testosterone tsunami. And I can vaguely recall my feelings of suicidal desolation back in 1968 when Mary Womack had other plans and couldn't go to see the brand new Steve McQueen movie, *Bullitt*, at the Granada Theater with me. Even so, I seriously underestimated the level of pure hormonal insanity that can bubble up when high school boys are in the same room with high school girls.

The way our programs operate, I go into a school along with a professional roots musician, and conduct workshops to help the kids learn to express themselves through the storytelling traditions of folk and blues music. To date I've worked with folk music icon Josh White, Jr. and singer/songwriter Kitty Donohoe, with help from acoustic blues master Robert Jones and harmonica virtuoso Peter Madcat Ruth.

First we put on a one-hour concert for the kids, who mostly think of Snoop Dogg as a minstrel poet from a bygone age, introducing them to the whole concept of folk and blues music. Then, with the help of the staff at the school, we recruit a group of kids to participate in six weeks of music writing workshops.

In the workshops we develop our song material by exploring what the kids have on their minds. Sometimes it's not all that much – here's the beginning of their modern ballad, "Puppy Poo:"

> *I woke up this morning*
> *Got out of my bed*
> *What's that squishin' between my toes*
> *"Aw, poo," I said...*

Other times, their thoughts are a little deeper, like the morning they were speculating on what might become of them after they got out of school:

It's dark out here, can't find the road
Feeling my way, through the bitter cold
I was safe and warm before
When I walked out that door
Nothin's gonna be the same anymore
I'm movin' on...

We also work with poems written by individual students:

A broken heart is a painful thing
Feel like an angel with a broken wing
Feel like a song no one can sing...

On the eighth week we put it all together into a professionally staged concert for all the students and staff in the school, with the kids participating in the performance as much as they are able. The look on their faces when they hear their peers and their teachers laughing at their silly ideas, or applauding some of their most deeply-held thoughts and feelings, is beyond anything I can describe. It's like watching a garden of roses bloom to the beat of an acoustic guitar.

Like I said, after all this time I'm still trying to catch my breath.

The song lyrics abstracted here were all written in the Lost Voices Roots Music Workshop at the Renaissance Alternative School in Howell, Michigan during January and February, 2008.

A Snowbird Snapshot

I just got home from a quick trip to Utah. This journey at the height of flu season involved riding for four hours each way packed into an airplane full of adults coughing like chain smokers running wind sprints, babies screaming between sneezes, and frightened Japanese tourists wearing surgical masks. It's a good thing I had my little bottle of hand sanitizer with me.

My trip involved going to a ski resort called Snowbird to speak and do some music for a conference. You know, about the only thing I can think of that is more fun than going to a ski resort in the Rocky Mountains in May is being paid to be there without having to bus tables in a Ski Bunny Sushi Bar.

It has been quite a few years since I spent any time in the Rockies, and the last time I was out there I wasn't exactly staying in the ritziest places.

On this trip, I had a room on the top floor of a first-class hotel called The Cliff, an amazing lodge right at the base of the slopes.

From my room I had a great view of the mountains, a panorama of most of the area's challenging and beautiful ski runs. I had the same terrific view from my shower, since the wall of the bathroom over the tub was a window. Of course, this also gave any skier who might happen to be interested a terrific view of me.

There was a Spa at the top of the hotel, with a well-equipped workout room, saunas, a rooftop outdoor lap pool and hot tub, a locker room you could host a wedding reception in, and a whole hallway of "treatment rooms."

The poster explaining the "treatments" at the Spa showed a picture of a woman lying on a table, wearing nothing but a towel and looking kind of dreamy, while another woman played some kind of solitaire tic-tac-toe on her bare back with a bunch of big, smooth black rocks.

The brochure touted "Bodywork: 11 varieties of massage including Swedish Massage, Couples Massage, Deep Tissue, LaStone® Therapy, Aromatherapy, High Altitude adjustment, Thai Massage, Shiatsu, Maternity Massage, Reflexology, and Seaweed Recovery Pack." It's good to know that if your seaweed should happen to need recovery, the Spa has a pack to take care of that.

I ran into some pretty interesting people in the Spa. Some were obviously rich folks who were able to spend a lot of time at Snowbird or resorts like it. You could recognize them by their expensive haircuts and Patek Philippe watches (apparently Rolex is for the unscrubbed masses).

These people, being skiers, typically had zero body fat, so the well-tanned skin of their faces stretched over their cheekbones like rawhide drum heads. Any time I gave one of them a friendly, "Hey! 'Sup?" they would merely raise one sun-bleached eyebrow over aristocratic pale blue eyes and stride off to their Shiatsu appointment.

The younger locals, mostly hotel employees, were a lot more fun. For one thing, they were skiers too, so they were also strong and fit, but they all had a nice healthy layer of beer fat. And since we were almost always in a situation where I might be giving them a tip at some point, they were generally willing to carry on a friendly conversation with the old guy.

In fact, they were almost always eager to tell me how they like to spend their off hours, along with the obvious skiing or snowboarding. It seems they all like to do things that make merely hurtling down a snow covered mountain with a 3,000 foot vertical drop on a pair of skis seem about as wild as getting one of those Maternity Massages.

A common pastime for these young daredevils is "Back Country Skiing," in which you spend three or four hours climbing up a sheer cliff with skis or a snowboard strapped to your back, then slide back down, staying just ahead of whatever avalanche or rock slide you happen to set off.

The only thing more astonishing than that is the fact that I spent four days in Utah, the reddest state in the Union, and I did not run into a single person who admitted to being a Republican.

It really is a brave new world!

A Matter of Kitchen Style

My wife and I recently went out on the old domestic limb and bought a new dishwasher.

It's not that we were unhappy with our old dishwasher; it ran just fine if we got up early to shovel the coal and let the boiler in the engine build up a good head of steam. Unfortunately, a clip broke on one side of the cup rack, and repairing it was going to involve replacing everything except one of the rawhide door hinges, so we decided that it was time to go shopping.

As you might have guessed, it's been a while since we bought an appliance, and we were shocked at some of the advances in technology. I figured that a logical first step would be to check Consumer Reports to find out which models would get all the crud off butter knives, and which ones were more likely to become sentient and destroy all human life.

The interesting thing about reading Consumer Reports is that their evaluators bring up a lot of things that never crossed your mind before. We have lived with our current dishwasher for more than eighteen years, and never once did I worry about how noisy it was. The theory has always been that any racket the thing could make is better than listening to me whining about hand-washing the dishes.

The reviews also talked a lot about how fast the dishwashers worked. Until now, my concept of dishwasher time has been that you started it, went away, and at some point in the future you would come back and the dishes would be clean. Now I found myself nodding with solemn approval at the model that was able to shave eleven seconds off the total job when using the pot scrubber mode by activating their unit's patented thermonuclear drying cycle.

One thing about which I had no doubt whatsoever was the color of the new dishwasher.

Let's just step aside for a minute here and have a little chat. Ordinarily, I would be about as concerned with the color of something like this as I am with the color of the drapes we have in the guest bedroom. At least, I assume we have drapes in there.

But a few years ago I had to replace the only "appliance" in the house I actually care about - my little gas grill, Bob. I replaced Bob with a modern masterpiece, a glittering behemoth that I lovingly call "The Enterprise." The Enterprise is made out of stainless steel!

Do you have any idea how emotionally fulfilling stainless steel is to a guy? It has a cool, technological vibe. It's industrial. It's powerful. It's the diametric opposite of the sissified taffy-colored ranges and refrigerators and dishwashers that minced around in my mother's kitchen.

Well, if they hadn't been inanimate objects, they would have minced.

So I was determined that I was not going to buy a mere dishwasher. I was going to bring our kitchen into the twenty-first century. I was going to own the Millennium Falcon with a pre-rinse option.

Strangely, my wife was slightly less passionate about that whole stainless steel thing. I think her exact words were, "There is absolutely no way we're getting stainless steel. None. Nada. Not a chance. Put it out of your mind. Not gonna happen. Uh uh. Nope." It turns out, stainless steel shows fingerprints. As she walked away I thought I heard her mutter, "Moron!"

My wife had decided that she wanted our dishwasher in a color called "Biscuit" - which is a sort of mincing "taffy" color. I was just going to have to forget about having an appliance that could make the Kessel Run in less than 12 parsecs. With a heavy heart, I headed for the store.

It didn't take long to find the perfect model, at the perfect price. But as we were finalizing the deal, the saleswoman told us that our ideal dish-washer was not available in Biscuit, even as a special order. But it could be had, at an even better price, in black.

And then the miracle happened. My wife said, "OK, no problem. Black would be nice." I could hardly believe my luck. We brought home the only thing in the universe that could be better than an under-counter Millennium Falcon.

We got Darth Vader!

Next up, installing Darth Vader.

Installing Darth Vader

In my last column I talked about our quest to buy a new dishwasher. In case you missed it, I was totally convinced when our adventure started that I knew exactly what I wanted - a futuristic study in stainless steel kitchen tech. Luckily, my wife was kind enough to explain that I was a complete idiot.

The whole episode turned out pretty well, though. We ended up finding just what we need- ed, and I inexplicably lucked out, ending up with a really super-cool black monolith of a dishwasher I call "Darth Vader."

When we bought Darth, the sales woman of- fered to have her store's experts install him in our kitchen for an additional $85. Since I already had a dishwasher the same size as the one we were buying, I thought to myself, "How hard can it be? Unhook the water, power, and drain from the old one, then hook 'em up to the new one. An hour at the most. $85? For that? Pah!"

I smiled jauntily at the sales woman and said, also jauntily, "Pah!"

It was going to take a week to get Darth delivered. This was ideal, since it would give me plenty of time to get the old dishwasher out and to prepare the space under the counter to receive the new one. My wife spent the week making sure that the plumber, electrician, a good carpenter, and a range of emergency medical services were all properly set up in the speed dial.

Almost immediately a little hitch came up. We've been in this house for eighteen years, and the old dishwasher had been here for at least ten years before that. I quickly discovered that nuts, bolts, washers and electrical connectors sort of petrify in place over that amount of time, so what I was doing was really more of an archeological dig. Still, with the help of my friend Scott, several cans of WD-40, and a few skinned knuckles, we managed to muscle the old dishwasher out of the kitchen and out onto the deck.

Peering into what would soon be Darth's Lair, it became obvious that the guys who installed the old dishwasher were mainly equipped with a couple of six packs and a lot of imagination. What they apparently did not have was a set of building codes. For instance, I was alarmed at the sight of eight seemingly random-sized chunks of pipe welded together to form the hot water feed.

But then I decided that the old dishwasher had worked just fine for a long, long time, so whatever Booze Brothers did way back then must have been all right. And besides, all the final fittings and connections were probably pretty standard. "Pah!," I thought.

Finally, the big day came. Looking back, I might have seen it as an omen that Darth's box was a tad larger than I had been planning for, and ripped the latch off the door-wall on the way in, but at the time I was too excited to care.

Darth came with a handy "Installation Kit," a large plastic bag containing an impressive selection of brass fittings, wires, connectors, hoses, and instructions. I particularly enjoyed the instructions, with headlines like, "!Avertissement!" over drawings of silhouette hands being sliced apart by moving parts, or fried by electrical current, or of silhouette installers being crushed to death by falling silhouette dishwashers.

Interestingly, not one of the brass fittings, wires, connectors, or hoses in the bag bore any relationship to all those "probably pretty standard" fittings and connections in the Lair. And the old wiring was about six inches too short. And the new dishwasher used a drain hose totally differ-ent from and incompatible with the old one. And the eight seemingly random-sized chunks of pipe welded together to form the water feed turned out to be anomalous in our physical universe.

It took seven trips to the hardware store and about twelve hours of work to get Darth properly settled in his Lair. I did not lose any fingers or toes, and not all that much blood. When my wife acted a little bit nervous about the first test run, I glow-ered at her and said, "I find your lack of faith... disturbing." She just rolled her eyes, pushed the "Start" button - and the dishes got clean!

So if you should happen to need a dishwasher installed, feel free to drop me an email with the word "Pah!" in the subject line. I'll find somebody to loan you the $85.

Darwin Rules

One day many years ago, when I was in college, I sat with a friend who happened to be a graduate student in anthropology, sipping a beer and gazing out the window at the ebb and flow of university life on the busy street below.

As we watched, a guy came hurtling out of the alley just up the street, squatting on a sort of land-surfboard made by replacing the legs on a rectangular coffee table with roller skates. This young inventor/athlete flew off the sidewalk and into four lanes of traffic, narrowly missing or being missed by every vehicle on the road in an almost unbelievable demonstration of pure good fortune.

Unfortunately, when he reached the curb on the far side of the street his luck pretty much ran out. Since there was no way to steer it or slow it down, his contraption hit the curb square-on at full velocity, levering the table top over the front wheels and turning it into a sort of coffee table trebuchet. The guy flew in a short, frantically-gesticulating arc across the sidewalk, through a plate glass shop window and into a display of leather handbags.

Since the scene was almost instantly under the control of paramedics whose ambulance was one of the vehicles the guy had narrowly missed, and a shop owner who was diligently caring for his handbags, my friend and I sat back and ordered another beer.

"What would make anybody try something like that?" I wondered.

"Well," he replied, "you've heard of Darwin's theory of evolution? What we have just witnessed is a member of our species trying really hard to chlorinate the gene pool."

Just this past weekend I was driving on the expressway and overtook a car that was speeding up, slowing down, and wandering from shoulder to berm in what appeared to be some sort of evasive action. Since it was early in the day, I assumed that this was an individual who might have enjoyed a margarita or two with that morning bowl of corn flakes.

I decided it would be best if the pending accident happened behind me, so as soon as I had a third lane to work with, I pulled up to pass. What

I discovered as I went by was a young woman driving with a small computer propped on the steering wheel, probably updating her Twitter status. I would say there is a real good chance that her last communication with our world will be 140 characters of immortal highway poetry:

OMG, I wnt a chsbugr so bad & its 8 miles to the next Brgr Kng. I thnk Emily has my lip gloss LOL, LOL, LOAAAAAAAAAAAAAAAArrrrrrrr rrrrrrrrrrrrrrrrrrggggggggggggggggggggh.

So what exactly is it that would make you check for gas leaks with a match? Or engage in a little target practice with your rifle by firing at a propane tank? What exactly is the thought process that would lead a person to raise rattlesnakes for fun and profit? Did you really think it was a good idea to go rollerblading at the end of a ski rope tied to the bumper of your buddy's Ford?

The answer to all these questions is simple; evolution. As my friend pointed out all those years ago, nature has a way of improving the species by weeding out the riff-raff.

In fact, this phenomenon is so well documented that Darwin Awards are given each year, "Honoring those who improve the human species... by accidentally removing themselves from it!" A recent Awardee is a Korean man who was so angered by missing an elevator that he rammed the doors with his wheelchair until they gave way, and he plunged to his death. If you have never seen the Darwin Awards, they make interesting, albeit pretty macabre, reading.

So the next time you see a man pumping gas with a cigarette hanging out of his mouth, take a moment to salute his dedication to the future of mankind - and move out of the blast radius.

Fight The Chill - Fire Up The Grill

For Michiganites, January means different things to different people. For some, it means tuning up the skis and heading to a resort for a few days of carefree fun, frolic, and compound fractures. For others, it's off to Florida to bask under a cloudy sky on a 45 degree day, then send smug postcards to the people they work with back home.

But for most of us, it means walking up an icy driveway from the mailbox with our Stupid Winter Hats perched on our heads, then skidding past the back door on one heel, clutching a handful of smug postcards from our coworkers in one hand and doing the "windmill prayer" (Oh God, Oh God, Oh God...) with the other.

But we Michiganonians are a hearty lot, and we try to make the best of the situation. A January afternoon breathing warm flower-scented air and gazing lovingly at the orchids at the Matthaei Botanical Gardens can remind us of all the abundant glories of nature, even while it revives that deeply hibernating case of hay fever.

A couple of hours at the Multiplex spent pretending that we are 10 foot tall blue guys living on a planet called Pandora will help us forget all about the weather outside, as well as troublesome real-life issues like the despicable actions of powerful corporations willing to despoil an entire planetary ecosystem for a little bit of profit.

Well, at least it will help us forget all about the weather outside.

But my favorite way to ward off these Ann Arbor winters is to grab a beer, mash up a couple of burger patties, and fire up the barbecue. For me, nothing recalls those wonderful idyllic days of summer like sitting back in a lawn chair and gazing at Whitmore Lake through a savory shroud of savory sirloin smoke.

OK, but before I am able to enjoy my seriously sibilant celebration of sizzles and suds, I have to shovel a path through the snow to get to the grill. Then I have to knock a crust of frozen crud off the vinyl grill cover and take it off really carefully so it won't crack from the cold. And sometimes I have to chip a little ice from around the edges of the lid of the grill before I can pry it open.

Of course, my stack of lawn chairs is always frozen solid, so I have to take a hair dryer and an extension cord out to melt one free. And instead of board shorts, sandals and a tank top, I have to wear a hoodie, a ski jacket, jeans, long johns, two pairs of socks, boots, a wool scarf, and a Stupid Winter Hat. With luck, I can usually make do without the whiteout goggles and snow shoes.

But other than those little details, the whole deal is just like a cookout in July!

Sitting by the grill in January, the things you see on the lake are actually a little bit like what you see out there in the summer. Instead of ski boats towing squealing kids on tubes, there are snowmobiles towing squealing kids on saucer sleds. Instead of fishermen sitting in big shiny bass boats and drinking themselves stupid on Jack Daniels, there are fishermen sitting in snug little ice fishing shanties and drinking themselves stupid on Jack Daniels.

You know, for a guy who started out in Hawaii, I have to admit that after 35 years in Michigan I kind of enjoy all this winter stuff. I like snow, I like ice skating, and I don't really mind talking to someone on the street while our words freeze in the air and clatter to the pavement. I've learned to lean into the season and truly embrace the idea of being a Michigaroonie.

Of course, it would be kind of fun now and then to have the chance to write a few smug postcards...

A note from the author - Please don't bother to write and tell me "It's Michigander." No, it's not. "Ganders" are male geese, so "Michiganders" would just make a lot of racket and crap all over your yard.

My New Beard

I grew a beard.

OK, I admit this is not exactly an accomplishment that's likely to earn me a Nobel Prize. Growing a beard is something pretty much any man can do, along with making those peculiar early morning sounds in the bathroom that have been emotionally scarring our wives and children for generations. Still, it means that I did accomplish something over the summer besides killing the grass.

I grew my beard so I could look a little bit more like one of my personal heroes, Pete Seeger, when I performed a musical tribute to him in July. Also, I figured that some new chin whiskers might take a little bit of attention away from my banjo playing.

As a child I thought beards were cool. My furry-faced idols ranged from Jesus Christ and

Abraham Lincoln to Ernest Hemingway and Santa Claus. Later, like every hippie from the 1960s, I developed a fascination with facial hair that was rooted in Elvis Presley's sideburns, refined through Sgt. Pepper's mutton chop madness, and culminated in ZZ Top's whatever-the heck-you-call-those-things.

This is not the first beard I've ever had. As a young man I experimented quite a bit with facial hair. Here are a few observations based on the results of my early research:

- One justification for growing a beard would be to save yourself the time and effort of shaving. This is only true if you go in for the basic "Wolf Man" or "Cousin Itt" look.

- A goatee takes at least as much work to maintain as being clean shaven. Plus, Star Trek has clearly shown us that wearing a goatee means that you are your own evil twin from an alternate universe. Or Satan.

- About the only thing a mustache accomplishes is to demonstrate that your body produces enough testosterone that you can grow one.

- A "soul patch" - that little dollop of hair just below the lower lip on an otherwise bare face that you see on some rock-and-roll musicians, baseball players, and mug shots of rapists - suggests that your body doesn't really produce all that much testosterone.

- Joe Miller, the maniac from Alaska who is running for the United States Senate, needs to either grow a beard or shave. Don Johnson and Chuck Norris wore out that whole "I'm just too busy and/or cool and/or stupid to sling a razor" look twenty-five years ago.

 - If you have a beard you should never, ever blow bubbles with your bubble gum. There are no exceptions to this rule.

So now I've ended my decades-long hairy hiatus. Interestingly (at least to me), my new beard is very different from the ones I had all those years ago. Back then, after a month or so of not shaving, I looked like I had fluffed up some old steel wool pads and pasted them randomly over my face. What a fantastic way to attract women that was!

My new beard is very different. Not only is it more evenly-distributed and tidy than before, it is about eighty percent gray, with an especially striking hint of "chin dipped in marshmallow sauce." After I recovered from the initial shock of seeing all that gray and discovering that I actually have aged, I found myself embracing the "grizzled old timer" thing. I have even started talking with a definite Gabby Hayes twang.

I'm not sure how long I'll keep the beard. It's pretty comfortable, easy to care for, and it doesn't seem to frighten too many animals or small children. As it goes with most things in my life, my wife will get the final vote. In that case, I guess I'll just go ahead and keep the beard until she notices that I've grown it.

Donna

Yesterday, one of my favorite people left our world behind.

Her name was Donna Lemon. She had a gentle voice, kind eyes, blue hair, and a sometimes unnervingly knowing smile. She also knew enough about finance and economics to fill the kind of books people carry around just so other people will think they are smart enough to actually read those books.

Since the day I moved in next door to Donna and her husband Harold, Harold and I have enjoyed a special friendship, something along the lines of the wise and infinitely tolerant elder and his younger protégé who doesn't know enough to keep his head out of the paint bucket.

Guess which one I was?

Harold and I had quite a few adventures over the years. We bought and restored a pontoon boat together. We dreamed up new and innovative ways to build docks. We ganged up on crabgrass and creeping Charlie. We drank pots of coffee and cases of beer.

And every time Harold and I would get to the point where one of us was trying to pry the paint bucket off the other one's head, Donna would show up carrying a plate of Oreos with the white stuff scraped off, blended with whipping cream and spooned back onto the cookies in perfect little swirls, and she would say, "I thought you boys could use a snack."

Donna always showed just that sort of grace in everything she did. She would never think of simply tossing a handful of carrots on a plate; she would be more likely to meticulously arrange them in a circle, alternated with blanched asparagus spears, and garnished with fresh herbs. Then she would bring her little culinary masterpiece out and offer it to Harold and me, standing waist-deep in the lake, where we would eat it with hands grease-caked from working on the pontoon boat's motor.

Donna never missed the opportunity to say a kind word, and if you did her even the slightest favor you could count on receiving a beautifully hand-written thank you note.

Donna and Harold were married for sixty-seven years. They raised one son. And a few years ago, when their only son tragically passed away, they stood strong against their grief and remained the kind of Grandparents that people write kids' books about.

They cultivated warm friendships from pretty much every place they went and everything they did, and I do not know one person who has ever met them who does not like and respect them.

I lost my mom and dad more than thirty years ago. Donna and Harold are right around the age my folks would be if they were still alive, and are exactly the kind of people that I would like to think my parents would have turned out to be. In fact, they are the kind of people I dream of turning out to be.

Donna did not want any sort of memorial service, any ceremony designed to make a fuss over her passing. Her plan was instead to wait for Harold, her husband, the man who spent nearly seven decades at her side, the man who held her hand to put a ring on it and who held her hand as she drew her last breath, to catch up with her.

And then she hoped that those of us who are left behind might take a little time to remember them both.

I guess that sounds about right. It is almost impossible to think about either one of them without thinking about the other one. And Donna always was willing to be patient, to the point of being a little bit stubborn.

When I started writing this column, I was worried that Donna might have thought of it as a kind of tribute, just the sort of thing she wanted us to avoid. But then I decided that she of all people would understand what it really is, a small reflection of the manners and good breeding she taught us all by example.

Thank you, Donna, for everything. Farewell.

Flu For Two

Well, it's another Autumn here in Michigan. Tigers fans are trying to get excited about watching the Yankees and the Phillies in the World Series; hunters are polishing their bullets and stockpiling Slim Jims in anticipation of Opening Day; soggy leaves are clogging up all the rain gutters; otherwise sane and rational mothers are wiggling into Slutty Firefighter, Slutty Pirate, or Slutty Investment Banker costumes for the neighborhood Halloween party; and the annual pitched battle over who is going to eat Thanksgiving dinner where and with whom is about to get underway.

Oh yeah, and Flu Season is here.

This year we are all excited about the H1N1 virus, better known as "Swine Flu." Not only is this an extremely virulent strain of influenza, especially dangerous and even life-threatening to children and pregnant women; it just sounds nasty.

I mean, think about it. It seems to me that adding the word "Swine" gives pretty much anything an unpleasant connotation. Could you really enjoy a "Swine Milk Shake?" On the other hand, "Playful Kitten Flu" seems like it might be kind of fun to have. You could even make the whole thing sound kind of whole-foods-healthy; just try saying "ToFlu" out loud.

So when I noticed the first sign of the Swine Flu (it's kind of like being whacked between the shoulder blades with a log splitter), I was resigned to enduring a few days of the galloping grungies. I banged down a couple of Alka-Seltzer Plus, put on a pair of sweat pants, some sweat socks and a sweat shirt, and settled down on the couch to do some serious sweating.

Now one thing every husband counts on when he is sick is being babied by his wife. We know that woman is by nature a sweet and nurturing creature, willing to treat a husband with the sniffles like a fallen warrior. The fallen warrior usually responds to his woman's kindness by becoming a whiney four-year-old for the duration.

So there I was, lying on the couch and noting with interest how my Swine Flu was grinding every muscle in my body, one by one, into pork sausage. At last I could hear my wife come home from work, so all the babying could commence. I took a deep breath and tried to work up my first coughing, hacking "Honnnneeeeeeyyyyy!"

Before I could make a sound, though, I got a good look at her. Her eyes were red and puffy as she stood weaving in the doorway, holding her purse strap loosely in one hand so that her bag dragged on the floor behind her. Her jacket was hanging off her shoulders, as if she had lacked the strength to get it all the way on. Her skin was roughly the color of guacamole.

Insightfully summing up the situation, I croaked, "Are you sick?"

"Unh-hunh," she said. "You?"

"Unh-hunh."

"Unh-oh!"

"Unh-hunh."

So we spent the next week groaning at each other across the living room while grocery bags full of used Kleenex accumulated on the carpet between us. Meals were a matter of trying to decide which one of us had the energy to make toast, then gathering enough strength to crawl out to the kitchen.

A small pharmacy sprang up on the coffee table, its top littered with a variety of over-the-counter remedies that promised much and mainly delivered a nasty aftertaste. We tried herbs and vitamins, washed down with Red Bush Tea. We drank bourbon with honey and lemon. We got some great cough syrup from the doctor that is the rough equivalent of hitting yourself on the head with a hammer - and I mean that in the best possible way.

We're both feeling quite a bit better now. At least we are able to trade coherent sentences and scramble a couple of eggs to go with the toast. But there is something about that week of shared misery that has drawn my wife and I closer together, forging a bond that somehow transcends everything that has gone before, and producing a deeper mutual respect and understanding.

Interestingly, my wife's recovery is a little bit ahead of mine. She is back on her feet, even back to work, and all-in-all demonstrating a lot more energy than I have. Hey, wait a minute. That means...

Honnnneeeeeeyyyyy!

Ask Dr. Mike - Tofurkey and a Lime Green Kilt

We haven't heard from our old friend Dr. Mike in quite a while. For new readers, Dr. Mike is an advice columnist whose main qualification for dispensing life-changing gems of wisdom is his Ph.D. in Melted Crayon Sculpture from the University of Tim Online ($29.95, two for $41.50). Here is what we found in this week's mail bag:

Dear Dr. Mike,

My wife's cooking is a lot more enthusiastic than it is edible. In fact, after word of her "Liver-Tofurkey Casserole Surprise" reached the Pentagon, she was hired as a consultant for the Army's Chemical War-fare Division.

Now she has invited my entire side of the family over to our house for a home-cooked dinner. My question is, could I be held responsible? I mean, isn't luring someone, especially a relative, into a known hazardous situation prosecutable in this state?

Signed,

Maybe I Should Cop A Plea

Dear Maybe,

I'm no lawyer, but as far as I am concerned anything involving Tofurkey should be at least a class-one felony. Go for the plea.

Dear Dr. Mike,

How dare you take my husband's side in criticizing my tofu-rrific cuisine. I'm a great cook, as all five of my late husbands would probably have testified.

I'll have you know that we had the dinner party my husband wrote you about, and his cousin Phil is expected to regain consciousness and partial use of his left hand, while the twins stand a good chance of recovering at least some of their sense of smell. Eventually. And Uncle Floyd says that Aunt Sadie probably would not have been around much longer anyway.

You slime-slinging scuzz-monkey.

PS - I'm your Biggest Fan,

The Wife Of The First Guy

Dear WOTFG,

On second thought, I'll change my advice to your husband. He would clearly be a lot safer on prison food. Please send my best wishes to Phil and the twins, and my condolences to Uncle Floyd.

Dear Dr. Mike,

You are probably going to think I'm crazy, but I feel like the clerks in clothing stores never treat me with proper respect. Whenever I go into Walmart and ask them to show me a new lime green kilt, they try to talk me into something I don't want - like pants. The same thing happens when I ask for top hats, two-tone wingtips or paisley lederhosen.

How do I get these people to stop passing judgment on me?

A big fan just like that last lady,

Wandering Through the Walmart Wilderness

Dear Wandering,

All I can tell you is that if the folks at Walmart think you have crappy taste, you should probably go ahead and re-examine your entire life strategy and value system.

In fact, if you consider Walmart a clothing store, I'd say you are pretty much off track to start with.

Good luck in your kilt quest.

Dear Dr. Mike,

Lately I find myself strangely drawn to the idea of taking all my clothes off and dancing the Tarantella on that little rim around the fireplace at Starbucks. Just for the record, I'm a 55 year old, 275 pound former University of Michigan linebacker.

Can you explain this compulsion?

Sincerely,

I'm Not Even Sure What The Tarantella Is

Dear Not,

No, I can't. Thanks for writing.

Well, that's it for this week. We invite all our readers to share their most personal problems with us, and get your life-changing advice from a guy who writes jokes for a living.

If you would like some help with a problem of your own, or if you just have a question, send an email to Mike@LearnedSoFar.com.

A Few Thoughts
About Mother's Day

Sunday is Mother's day. This is a holiday during which the men of America team up with their children to treat Mom to a sumptuous breakfast in bed, featuring chocolate chip waffles and grapefruit juice. Having no idea where Mom keeps the coffee beans, Dad and the kids run Hamster Kibbles through the coffee grinder, figuring "What the heck, how bad could it be?"

After breakfast the family watches excitedly as Mom unwraps the 21-piece non-stick skillet set they bought her from Costco, laboring under the assumption that non-stick skillets are exactly what she dreams about all day, every day, in her office at the law firm.

Of course there are the commercial Mother's Day cards, with pictures of flowers and heartfelt messages like:

Mom, you're beautiful and fragrant;
You've helped us grow from boys to men.
Without you, Dad would be a vagrant;
Oops, the cat puked in the Den.

Afterward, Mom can reflect fondly back on her special day as she chips the dried-up chocolate chip waffle batter off the kitchen ceiling.

It is only right that we take a little time now and then to honor the mothers of the world. They give birth to us, nurse us, change our diapers, teach us just about everything we know before we start school, and occasionally talk Dad out of shooting us or selling us off to be used for scientific experimentation.

So just what is it that makes a woman want to be a mother? I'm guessing that it would not be the physical sensation of childbirth, which my wife described as the rough equivalent of pooping a watermelon. And it doesn't seem likely that it would be the promise of rolling out of bed in the middle of the night every time a young child is hungry, or sick, or frightened, or bored, or stinky, or thirsty, or lonely, or...

Could it be the excitement of the phone call from the first grade teacher wondering where her child learned a particular word that she was teaching to all the other kids at recess? How about the thrill of driving her ten year-old to the emergency room for stitches - again? Or staying up all night before the Science Fair helping her seventh grader rebuild his project after that little misunderstanding involving the fire department and the EPA?

Maybe she looks forward to sitting up all night waiting to hear what's left of the car pulling into the driveway the first time her son borrows it for a date. Or trying to convince her daughter that she may want to reconsider dating that guy with the tattoos and the stove bolt through his ear, the one who works at the 7-Eleven now that he's out on parole.

Is it skipping lunches so she can afford to pay for her son's wedding rehearsal dinner? Or having to bite her tongue when she finds out that her daughter's idea of the perfect wedding involves a Buddhist priest, some farm animals, and a skydiving Elvis?

Or maybe it's the day she will have to bury her tears as she watches her child proudly wearing a uniform, waving good-bye as he heads out to a place where he will fight for his country - and for her.

Maybe it is all of these things, along with the countless other Mommy Moments that, somehow, eventually add up to the young adults who will one day take over the world. All I can say is, I'm sure glad that all those moms are crazy enough to want to do the job. So take a little time and thank them.

There are a lot of people like me, who can no longer send our moms a card or hand them a cup of Kibble coffee. All we can do is hold them in our hearts and our memories, and feel a little bit bad about all the torment we put them through, and smile.

Moms always do like to see us smile.

Father's Day Again

When my son was in about second grade, he made me a bookmark that features a sort of ransom note version of the words "Happy Fathers Day." The paper is bright orange (his favorite color at the time), and his teacher laminated the finished product in clear plastic to protect it from the beer and coffee stains we fathers can be counted on to get all over our things.

My son, who is now twenty-nine years old and has been out of second grade for a while, might be surprised to learn that I still have that bookmark - although, at the moment it is stuck in one of the stack of books I'm working my way through, and I haven't seen it in a couple of weeks.

There are a few names I have been called in my life that I really enjoy. "Honey" is fun when you get it from a super friendly (and usually equally voluminous) waitress in a Waffle House, and even better from the woman you've been married to for nearly 35 years. "Mate" is nice when spoken by either my friend from Australia or my friend from Cornwall, England. "Coach" is great to be called by a bunch of sincere and smelly little hockey players flopping around an ice rink at 6:30 in the morning.

But the best thing I've ever been called is, "Father." Likewise, "Dad," "Pop," "Daddy," "Papa," and even, under the right circumstances, "Old Man."

So now all of us Old Men are bracing ourselves for Father's Day and the annual onslaught of sincerely-bought humorous barbecue aprons, sincerely-chosen humorous greeting cards, and if we are very, very fortunate, sincerely-made lopsided coffee mugs that made it out of the kiln just in the nick of time before Summer Break.

The weekend has already started off with a fair amount of excitement. On Friday night we had a storm with "near hurricane-force winds," which was for the most part pretty entertaining. The power went out right away, giving us the opportunity to play with candles. The lightning was really festive without hitting any of our stuff, and the whole thing scared the hairballs out of Libby the Psychotic Cat. What could be better than that?

On the downside, when we went out Saturday morning we discovered that a big chunk of the neighbor's maple tree had squished the roof of Nan's car, "Gracie."

As I was out there in the driveway, sweeping up splintered bits of maple tree and Gracie and wondering when the power might come back on, I realized that I was completely immersed in my "Dad" element; like most guys, I'm never happier than when I'm horsing around with something inanimate.

Once I got my own wreckage under control, I took some time to wander around the rest of our storm-tossed little town. Everywhere I went, I saw women standing in little groups and talking quietly, sharing their feelings about the storm or their losses, or at least making sure that everyone had all the details straight.

At the same time the men were happily swarming over the downed trees with chain saws and axes. Taking care of the inanimate stuff. Not much conversation going on, but a whole lot of noise.

And I realized that this was a great way to explain why moms like to get flowers for Mother's Day, while all us dads are hoping for a power drill. You see, moms are always on duty to take care of the bruised shins and broken hearts. They kiss all the boo-boos and make them better.

Dads are in charge of the sump pump.

And you know what? That seems to work out just fine for everyone. Happy Father's Day, guys!

There's Just Something About the Solstice

This past week we celebrated the Summer Solstice, the longest day of the year. To farmers this represents the midpoint of the growing season, halfway between planting and the harvest. To Catholics it means that the solemn Feast of Saint John The Baptist is just a few days away. And of course, for all you druids out there, it's Party Time!

Each year more than 28,000 people show up at Stonehenge on England's Salisbury Plain to stand watch until the first dawn, when the golden rays of the morning sun will emerge in perfect alignment with the giant stone astronomical "computer," as they have on that sacred site for nearly 6,000 years. Of course, this "seeing the first rays of the sun" thing is purely theoretical, since the last cloudless morning in England is rumored to have occurred in 1089 AD, during the reign of William II (also known as Rufus the Red or, to the workers in the Royal Laundry as Butthead the Incontinent).

Still, it appears that the neo-pagans over at Stonehenge got into the spirit of the thing and consumed enough neo-brewskis that they hardly noticed a little bit of Rain on the Salisbury Plain.

There are no details available about any kind of organized celebration on this side of the pond at Carhenge, the faithful (more or less) replica of Stonehenge constructed from thirty eight cars sticking trunk-down out of the high plains near Alliance, Nebraska. One can only imagine the breathtaking sight of the dawn breaking in perfect alignment over the hood of a 1962 Cadillac.

Here in Whitmore Lake, the day was marked by an armada of small boats anchored on the sand bar throughout the day and evening, their occupants celebrating the most spiritual aspects of the solstice by ritually consuming many gallons of Budweiser, Mike's Hard Lemonade, and highly mystical potions like the sacred "Jaeger Bomb." This giant floating party was accompanied by laughter, festive music, and a strangely rapid rise in the temperature of the lake.

Ok, please don't bother sending me letters or emails to say, "Ewwwwwww." There is absolutely no actual proof that this lake-al warming has anything to do with human activities. Didn't you ever hear of volcanoes... in Whitmore Lake?

Overall, this year's party was what could best be described as "heroic." We enjoyed the delicious scent of brats sizzling on boat-mounted grills, blending with the bacon-like aroma of Whitmore Lakians sizzling in the sun. The shrieks of young women suddenly discovering ice cubes in their bikinis (or the sudden loss of key parts of their bikinis), merging with the dulcet tones of Kid Rock singing "All Summer Long" through the 1000 watt sound system on some guy's brand new wakeboard boat with his speakers operating at the approximate decibel output of a 747 engine.

So now that the solstice is past, we can get down to some serious business. All the swim rafts are anchored out in the water, the tubes are inflated, the water skis and wake boards are out of mothballs, and the flip-flops are out of those weird flat storage boxes under the bed. The "noodles," beer koozies, and floating ice chests are tuned up and ready for a season of "flinking" (floating and drinking). The ski boats have begun to collect their annual wads of fish line on the props, while the fishermen are surfing the internet to see if anyone has yet come up with a freshwater Naval mine designed specifically to take out ski boats.

Welcome back, Summer!

A Tale of a Tomless Dock

One of the things that happens here on the lake every time winter goes into remission and we catch a dose of springtime is that we have to cobble together some sort of a dock. Having a dock gives us a way to walk out to the boat all summer without getting our flip-flops wet.

For the past fifteen years my main dock-slinging sidekick has been my friend Tom. Over this past winter Tom decided to desert the Ann Arbor area and move to Arizona, since it offers better weather, more employment opportunities, and the right to carry a handgun without a permit - or any conceivable reason to do so. And the only downside is that, since he's from England, he will have to have his papers in his pocket at all times, or he could wind up enjoying the weather in Tijuana.

So Tom's departure left building the dock pretty much up to my son Pat and I. We chose a weekend not long after the thaw, our theory being that as we worked our way through the project the lake would be cold enough that we could use it to ice down our beer - along with any contusions, abrasions, burns, or minor fractures that might crop up.

My son, who up until the time he moved away from home had never so much as picked up a screwdriver, now works for a company that designs and makes power tools. This means that he showed up on Dock Day armed with an assortment of laser-guided levels and other space-age gadgets. And he knew right where the power switches were on every one.

One of the tools he brought along is called a "Hammerhead." This battery-operated Hammer of the Future can easily drive a nail that would require about 3 good swats with a regular hammer, only it does it in less than 50 seconds at 35 strikes per second. This means that you get something like 1750 ear-splitting bangs out of every nail.

In other words, this is the coolest tool I have ever seen!

Since the dock is mostly put together with screws, nuts, and bolts, we couldn't find much use for the Hammerhead there. So after we used up the charge on the battery blasting the bejesus out of any loose nails we could find around the house, we reluctantly put it aside and spent the rest of the morning playing with all the other tools.

After lunch, we ran down the battery in the Hammerhead again, then diligently tucked right into the dock. We got two sections placed and leveled before we realized that there was no way to connect any of the other sections to them.

You see, after the fifteen years Tom and I spent tinkering that dock together, at this point it is pretty much a jigsaw puzzle. Anyone who has ever done a jigsaw puzzle can tell you that if even one piece is out of place, it screws up everything else so that it never quite looks like the picture of a cute little white kitten in a laundry basket that's on the cover of the box. Plus, you can't tie your boat to it.

After spending an hour or so standing around wearing waders and frowns, I remembered that Tom had, in a moment of inspired madness, shot a picture of the entire finished dock and labeled each section. I dug out the photo and we started over, following that picture like it was the blueprint for an F/A 18 fighter jet.

We eventually got the dock all put together, and managed to do it with hardly any life-threatening injuries or frostbite. Although, I'm pretty sure that toward the end there we had the power turned up a little bit high on the laser level, and we sank a passing Bayliner.

So Tom, I'm glad you're enjoying Phoenix, and you'll be happy to know that we're muddling through pretty well back here. But we do miss you, Mate.

Ernie

I moved to Southeast Michigan on a blind date in the Spring of 1975. When I arrived I was a White Sox fan, mostly because I had spent my formative high school years within easy obscenity-shouting distance of Chicago. Back in those days, probably the best thing about our pathetic Sox was a broadcaster named Harry Caray, who was known for saying "Holy Cow!" Harry used this as a fairly transparent substitute for shouting obscenities.

As that first summer unfolded, two amazing things happened that more or less reshaped my life. First, Nan and I decided that the blind date was going well enough to go ahead and get married, which is bound to make a summer stick in your mind, just about any way you cut it.

Second, I discovered the amazing voice of a Detroit Tigers baseball play-by-play man named Ernie Harwell.

Ernie was already a seasoned professional broadcaster back in 1960 when he came to work for the Tigers. He had started doing radio broadcasts of major league baseball games for the Brooklyn Dodgers in 1948, after he was picked up on a trade with the Atlanta Crackers for catcher Cliff Dapper. This launched Ernie on what was to become a Hall of Fame broadcasting career, and it gave Dapper the unfortunate distinction of being the only professional baseball player in history to be traded even-up for a microphone jockey.

So by the time I first heard Ernie holler, "That ball is LOOOOONG GONE!" after a home run, he had already called something like 2,300 major league ball games. He pretty much knew what he was doing.

Now a baseball game is just about perfectly designed for radio. You have occasional bursts of gentle and easily-described action, separated by really long periods of time during which coaches and players carry on silent conversations using cryptic (and generally pretty comical) hand signals, scratch themselves in places only a guy would tackle in public, and spit tobacco juice.

This leaves a whole lot of air time for discussing obscure statistics, telling homespun anecdotes, and making bucolic observations about pretty much anything. And this is precisely where Ernie was maybe the best who ever sat down behind a microphone. He seemed to know a little something about everybody in baseball, and always had wonderfully insightful stories to tell.

Then there was The Voice. Ernie had the natural speaking rhythm and tone of a grandfather, the really cool one who could always tell you a story to make you smile, and feel comfortable, and believe that at that moment the world is exactly as it was meant to be.

He came to work at the ballpark each day with a verbal tool box of Ernie-isms that I never got tired of hearing. If a batter took a called strike, Ernie would be likely to say, "...he stood there like the house at the side of the road and watched that one go by." He would describe a double play as "...two for the price of one for the Tigers." Of course, with his faint Atlanta drawl he always pronounced it "Taggers."

If a foul ball went up into the crowd he would inform us that, "A young man from Lake Orion (or Traverse City, or Mason, or Port Huron, or whatever) caught that one." I wonder how he always knew?

During that first summer in Michigan, and for about the next twenty summers after that, I spent nearly every evening with my little transistor radio, listening to Ernie tell us that "...the pitcher and catcher are having a confab at the mound," or,

"...that last pitch just caught the outside corner - Mr. Chylak said so." And I treasured every word.

I met Ernie Harwell in person once. It was toward the end of his career, and he was all alone walking along the concourse near the press box in Tiger Stadium wearing a Greek fisherman's cap. I was struck by how small a man he was, and by the intelligent kindness in his eyes. I introduced myself, shook his hand, then babbled on and on about how much I loved listening to him.

He listened patiently and thanked me for my kind words. Then he basically interviewed me, asking all sorts of questions about my column and my life, listening to each answer as if I was somehow the most important person he could possibly be talking to, rather than a star-struck fan who had accosted him in front of the hot pretzel stand.

A few years back Ernie retired from broadcasting. True to form, in his good-bye comments he knew just the right words to help all of us deal with the end of an era that we had hoped would somehow go on forever. Here is my favorite part:

"Thank you for letting me be part of your family. Thank you for taking me with you to that cottage up north, to the beach, the picnic, your work place and your backyard.

"Thank you for sneaking your transistor under the pillow as you grew up loving the Tigers.

"Now I might have been a small part of your life. But you have been a very large part of mine. And it's my privilege and honor to share with you the greatest game of all."

Ernie, your natural humility may lead you to think of it like that, but I'm here to say that you were a far greater part of all our lives than you may be willing to imagine. And now as you move on to your next great adventure, you should know that we are all better, richer, and happier because you were kind enough to spend all those years chatting with us.

So thank you Ernie. We will never forget you.

35 Years of Tigers

A couple of weeks ago my family made our first trip to Comerica Park to see a Detroit Tigers game. I have to admit that while we are all long-time Tiger fans, I have not been in a big hurry to go down there - and only partly because I resent having to take out a home equity loan to swing the down payment on a couple of plastic cups full of lukewarm beer.

My biggest issue with Comerica Park is that I really loved the old Tiger Stadium, a place where you could save a few dollars and buy "obstructed view" seats. This meant sitting directly behind a steel I-beam support, so pretty much all you would see of the game was that beam and the hot dog vendor.

Even so, there was always a lot of noise in that old park, the hot dogs were pretty good, and on your way in and out you got to feast your eyes on the greenest green you'll find anywhere in the world - Tiger Stadium grass.

I think part of the attraction was the history of the place. The first ballpark built at the corner of Michigan and Trumbull was Bennett Park, carved in 1895 out of an old-growth forest. The management at the time was way out ahead of the curve on that whole idea of obstructed view seating, since they decided to leave eight of the biggest elm and oak trees in the outfield.

In 1912, when they remodeled the park for the new century and named it Navin Field, they took out the trees and installed a 125 foot flag pole in center field that set a record as the tallest obstacle ever built in fair territory in a major league ball park. For years the charm of watching a game from the bleachers was made even better by the occasional crunching thud of a center fielder smashing into that flag pole.

I should point out that I did not become a Tiger fan until I moved to Michigan in the mid-1970s and fell in love with that old ball park. Back then the Tigers themselves were pretty much an acquired taste, like drinking Irish whiskey or having a mule kick you repeatedly in the side of the head. You see, the Tigers had won a World Series in 1968, and something in that experience apparently convinced them that they would be better off if they were to almost completely avoid winning anything at all for about the next fifteen years.

By the mid-'70s Detroit's success-oriented fans were staying away from the Tigers in droves, which in turn meant that my wife and I could usually wander down to Tiger Stadium on just about any day and drop a few dollars on great seats to a game featuring the strange and wonderful assortment of lunatics that made up the Tigers' roster.

In those wonderful days the Tigers had a first baseman named Norm Cash, who once came to bat against Nolan Ryan swinging a table leg.

They also had a wonderful third baseman named Aurelio Rodriguez, who was always smiling, and who could throw a ball over to first at a little over Mach 4, but who might as well have been swinging a badminton raquet at the plate. He was from Mexico, and in interviews he sounded exactly like the old Saturday Night Live parody of the Latin ball player; "Baseball 'been 'berry, 'berry good to me."

Al Kaline, one of the greatest right fielders of all time, retired in 1974 and become a broadcaster. In 1971 Kaline had turned down a raise that would have given him the first $100,000 salary in Tigers history, saying that he didn't feel that he had played well enough that year to earn it. In 1972 he played a lot better and took the dough.

There was a pitcher named John Hiller, who once showed up sporting a nasty-looking Fu Manchu and a shaved head just to psych out batters, and another one named Dave Rozema who messed up his knee and probably his career trying to execute a flying kung-fu kick during a bench-clearing brawl.

And then there was Mark "The Bird" Fidrych. My wife and I happened to be sitting behind third base on the evening Fidrych made his first home start, crawling around on his knees to groom the mound, talking to the ball, and bounding around the infield to congratulate teammates for making nice plays. He also threw the liveliest fastball I've ever seen, and he had a truly diabolical slider.

After one loony but brilliant season, The Bird tore his rotator cuff trying to pitch on a bad knee, and never made it back to major league form. The gentle grace and good humor he used to deal with his too-short career made his accidental death earlier this year seem all the more tragic.

Over the years I got to see a lot of baseball and even another World Series victory in Tiger Stadium. Some of the players were great, some just greatly interesting; Alan Trammell, John B. Minivan, Lou Whitaker, Rusty Minivan, Kirk Gibson, Jack Morris, Lance Parrish, Cecil Fielder, Todd Jones and many others. Now, the Stadium and all those guys are gone from the game.

Ok, I'll admit it - Comerica Park is really nice. There are good restaurants, real bathrooms, a Ferris wheel, and no obstructed view seats. The Tigers of today are all fine professional athletes as well as certifiable characters in their own right, and they seem to know quite a bit more about winning than the guys in the '70s did.

The grass in Comerica is pretty green, too. Maybe it's not the greenest possible green that it was all those years ago at the corner of Michigan and Trumbull, but I guess I can try to get used to it.

Speaking Of Cleavage

OK, this is going to come as a shock to a lot of you. It is not the kind of thing I ordinarily discuss here. In fact the only reason I'm doing it at all is that, now that the new iPhone has solved every problem of mankind, there is not really all that much for us to talk about. So here goes:

Men look at women! They do it a lot!

I know, right?

And the thing is, when we do it, we are apparently just responding to our genetic programming. In hundreds (probably) of psycho-neurological studies (why not?), it has been proven (let's assume) that a man's response to visual stimulation is almost completely involuntary.

Yeah, that's the ticket.

What this boils down to, in layman's terms, is that guys just can't help looking at girls - especially when it comes to the idea of getting a peek at the "naughty bits.:

But I have to tell you that this is a two way street. Here in our new age, women are taking advantage of the uplifting technological advances that have pushed up and into the forefront of our cultural milieu.

In case you are completely innuendo-impaired, what I'm talking about here is the "Wonderbra" and the rise (sorry) of cleavage as a modern fashion phenomenon. The Wonderbra has elevated us (OK, I'll stop now) into an era of partially exposed breasts such as we have not seen since (according to eminent French cultural historian Mel Brooks) Louie XIV said, "It's good to be the king!"

Here's how I figure it works; men like to watch women, and women like to watch men watching them. So those women will spend $34.95 (on sale) to make the whole thing happen.

But women seem to have a problem with men when "watching" crosses the line, sneaks right on past "leering" and goes straight into "ogling." The thing is, us guys have kind of a hard time with subtle distinctions like that. Remember all that crap about genetic programming?

Not too long ago I experienced what it feels like to be ogled. As I was walking through a restaurant, I noticed two attractive ladies staring at me "below the waist." They were whispering to each other, hiding their words behind their hands, and giggling lasciviously.

I was shocked! I began to feel a slow burn of indignation that these women might value my physical attributes over my mind or my personality. I resented being objectified in that way. I felt totally used.

I also made a mental note of which pants I was wearing, so I could buy some more just like them.

I was still steaming about it when I got back to the table, where my wife pointed out that I had come out of the Men's room with a wad of my Pink Panther boxer shorts zipped into and hanging out of my fly.

But that's not exactly the point. For a brief moment in that restaurant, I understood what a woman must feel like when, after putting on an outfit that pops something like thirty percent of her bosom out into the world, the men around her notice that they can see nearly a third of her bosom.

With this in mind, I have decided to put my new found insight to work. I want men to learn how to look at women, while still respecting their dignity and almost completely avoiding getting tased.

Next time: To See, Or Not To See; The Modern American Man's Field Guide to Looking Without Actually Ogling.

To See, or Not to See;
*The American Man's Field Guide to
Looking Without Actually Ogling*

Last week I mentioned that men can't help looking at women, especially when a little bit of cleavage is involved. I admit that this is about as startling as saying that the sun rises in the East or that Glenn Beck is daisy-plucking, talking-to-imaginary-hummingbirds crazy.

Still, it had to be said.

Now we are going to explore ways for men to follow their natural instinct to peek without getting pepper sprayed.

To start with, try to understand that to some extent this is all mostly a matter of being polite. A woman, unlike a man, generally has a pretty good idea what she is wearing and what it looks like. And unless she was raised by wolves (female ones), you can be fairly sure that she knows about guys and cleavage.

This means that if she has The Girls on display, she pretty much expects any normal healthy guy to look. It's just that, having that pesky female tendency toward subtlety and nuance, she doesn't want you to look too much.

So step one is to try not to be completely obvious. When catching that first tantalizing glimpse, you should avoid doing a triple-take, stomping your foot, flapping your arms and shouting, "Za-za-za zowie!" My guess is that this is just the sort of thing that would be considered "over the line."

Instead, stay calm. Take a few deep breaths. Keep your eyes above the neck while you regain your composure and develop some sort of strategy. You might want to try to find and concentrate on a unique feature on the woman's face to help you stay focused, like a mole or her Maori battle tattoo.

You have to be a little bit careful not to linger too long in this phase. If you just stand there staring at that Maori battle tattoo and completely ignoring The Girls, she will begin to think either that you are deranged, or that she has a chunk of spinach in her teeth. So take your time, but get on with it.

A main element of your plan should be deception. This might be something as simple as wearing a pair of sunglasses. Those big old "Billy Bob The Deputy Sheriff Who Gave You A Ticket Just Outside Diphtheria Springs, Alabama" mirrored aviators are especially good for this. They will let you go ahead and stare away while she touches up her mascara in the reflection.

If you are not already wearing sunglasses, though, you might find it awkward to run out to the car to get them. Especially if it's nighttime. If you can't come up with some logical alternative, like putting on a handy pair of cardboard 3-D glasses or a welder's mask, you'll have to resort to misdirection.

The object of misdirection is to get the woman looking at something else long enough for you to grab your peek. Try shouting something like, "Say, isn't that Christian Bale over there showing Johnny Depp and Orlando Bloom how to play beach volleyball?"

Well, how do you know she'll never buy it, if you don't try it?

The important thing to remember is not to be greedy. Once you've had your look, go ahead and move along to the next level of interpersonal discourse. Like, just to throw out a totally radical alternative, you could engage in some sort of con-structive, meaningful conversation.

I know it sounds crazy, but it's crazy enough that it just might work.

Flying Blind

Everybody knows that the airlines have not been doing that well lately. Between the rising cost of fuel and the ongoing hassles of cleaning up after young Nigerian millionaires with exploding underpants, the industry has been faced with a series of unprecedented challenges.

To add insult to injury, a certain volcano erupted in Iceland. The volcano is called, I'm not kidding, "Eyjafjallajokull," which is really hard to say for most news reporters; it's actually pronounced "Xgicxgsrnlglu." The cloud of ash launched into the air by Eyjafjallajokull shut down airports all over Europe and paralyzed air travel world-wide. Of course, most airlines are not compensating the stranded passengers in any way, since a volcano is an "Act of God."

Still, their profits are in trouble. Things are getting so grim that the airlines may eventually have to let the average income of their top executives plunge below three million dollars a year!

OK, funny story:

Last fall I had a ticket to fly to New York on an airline that shall remain nameless (let's just call them "Delta"). This trip was something I really wanted and needed to do; it was a great business opportunity, plus it would provide me with a chance to recharge my creative batteries, strolling the urine-soaked streets of the greatest (or at least the most urine-soaked) city on Earth.

Unfortunately, a couple of days before the flight I noticed a slightly uncomfortable feeling between my shoulder blades. It was a little bit like having my spine torn out with a corkscrew. Within an hour my throat felt like I had been swallowing broken glass, my lungs were turning themselves inside out, and my head had cracked open from the inside. I had come down with a touch of what is commonly called the "Swine Flu."

Now I know how much all air travelers admire a fellow passenger who has the dedication to bravely leave his sick bed and fly, despite coughing chunks of his pancreas onto the eyeglasses of the woman sitting next to him on the plane. I guess I just do not have that kind of dedication, so we contacted the nameless airline (Delta) and told them that I was too ill to fly.

They informed us that, while the ticket was non-refundable, because we were dealing with an unavoidable illness - which many people might very well call an "Act of God" - we could apply the cost of the ticket to a future flight - is there anything else we can help you with today, and thank you very much for choosing their nameless airline ("Delta").

Fast-forward to a couple of weeks ago. We had another New York trip scheduled, and I thought, "Gosh! Wouldn't this just be a Jim-dandy time to use that old ticket to New York! Why don't we just call up that nameless airline ("Delta"), and I'm sure they will be happy to take care of everything."

OK, so here's where it really gets hilarious.

Getting through to a human being at this particular airline that shall not be named ("Delta") is pretty challenging. They have installed a state-of-the-art automated phone system, in which a computer with a sexy voice asks a long series of questions to determine what you need, listens carefully to each of your answers, then disconnects your call.

But I can be pretty persistent, and not all that judicious with my time. I eventually got through to an agent who informed me that, according to her records, I had in fact traveled to New York last fall. I told her that on that date I was not able to travel to the bathroom without help, so I'm pretty sure I would have remembered making it all the way to 7th Avenue and 34th Street.

After a little more discussion she went on to admit that my return ticket had not been used. Apparently, the nameless airline ("Delta") thought that I had decided to stay in the Big Apple, and was now living in a walk-up in Soho.

The bottom line of our conversation was that I would have to drive to the airport, find a ticket counter for the nameless airline ("Delta"), and swear before God and a Gate Agent that I had not used that ticket. If I did this they would transfer the ticket, keeping a $150 penalty fee (out of $250).

It's uncanny. It's almost as if they knew that the fuel, parking and time would cost me more than $100!

So here it is. I'm wondering how a simple columnist like me, who only talks to thousands of people in airline markets all around the country, should go about asking this nameless airline (Delta) what the difference is between their "Act of God" (remember that unpronounceable volcano?) and my "Act of God."

Any ideas?

Fly the Fiendly Skies

Last week I wrote about my less-than-satisfactory experience as a customer of a major airline that probably should not be named (it was Delta). What that experience came down to was that the airline (Delta) basically told me that they had my money, and they dared me to try to get anything in return for it.

The amount of feedback I got on this one suggests that I am far from the only traveler who has been cast adrift in what one reader called the "parallel universe of airline logic." For instance, I learned from a reader who is a travel agent that most airlines will not pay a travel agency any commission for selling a seat on one of their planes, but they will send them a bill if they should make a mistake doing it.

So after my less-than-satisfactory experience with that one airline (Delta), we booked last month's New York trip on a different unnamed airline (Spirit) - and discovered a whole new way to think about the words "customer service."

This new airline (Spirit) has adopted a sort of "water torture" method of extracting money from customers, one drip at a time. They sell you a really cheap ticket, then charge fairly stiff fees for everything involved in actually going on your trip; checked luggage, carry-on bags, pre-selected seats. They even charge about three dollars for one of those little bags of nuts.

Now please don't think that I completely lack sympathy for the airlines. As I pointed out last week, their top executives make just over three million dollars a year on the average. This means that these people shockingly live in an income bracket where they have to think twice about ordering the solid platinum shower curtain rings for the vacation place in Maui, and many of them end up making do with the 24K gold ones.

So to help these poor suffering executives keep their basement mini-fridges stocked with Beluga Caviar, I decided to come up with a few suggestions to help them boost their profits:

1. Charge extra for not getting a seat between a hippie with a head cold and a 350 pound guy named "Snake" who believes that personal hygiene is for sissies.

2. How about a "Seat Belt Surcharge?" You could ding each passenger a dollar or two to buckle up. Then when you land, you could charge them ten bucks to get out.

3. Take the lap belt concept to the next level; in the unlikely event of sudden loss of cabin pressure, an oxygen mask would drop down from the overhead - just as long as you have a valid major credit card on file.

4. Charge a fee to use the rest room. This would be especially effective if you were serving a population who might be inclined to, say, drink a few beers.

5. Replace those decadently luxurious coach-class airline seats with bar stools. You could cram twice as many people into the same space, plus you would achieve a festive "happy hour" mood that could seriously boost restroom revenues. OK, I admit that it might be sort of dicey hanging onto a bar stool while the plane accelerates to or stops from 200 miles per hour. But as long as your credit card holds out, you could invest in that optional lap belt.

6. To heck with bar stools - go ahead and pack those planes with standing room only!

Interestingly, as you read these words, some real airlines are actually trying to implement those last three ideas. In Ireland, an airline called Ryanair is working on both pay toilets and budget bar stool seating. It's bound to work; who ever heard of an Irishman sliding off a bar stool?

And Spring Airlines in China is just waiting for regulatory approval to start offering a discounted fare for standing room service. Spring officials say that an important aspect will be a safety belt fastened around the passenger's waist. It is not clear to me just how this is going to work, but I think I would pay extra to not have old Snake strapped in behind me.

When we were coming home from New York, the flight attendant told us how she had been trained to think about her employer (remember Spirit?). She said that her boss told her, "Don't get all excited about the job. We are nothing more than a Greyhound bus attached to a 7-11."

Does anybody besides me think that represents a pretty nasty insult to Greyhound and convenience stores everywhere?

Harold

I consider myself a really lucky guy. In my career I've had the opportunity to write all kinds of things, most of them silly, and writing them has usually been fun. But every now and then I have had to put the silliness aside and say goodbye to a friend.

Just a little over seventeen years ago our family threw all our stuff in boxes, threw the boxes in a truck, and headed up the road from Ann Arbor to move into a house on the shores of Whitmore Lake. The house came with nice carpeting, a great view of the water, and a neighbor named Harold.

Harold was about 75 years old when I first met him. He was hobbling around his back yard with a cane, and in our first conversation he told me that he was just about to go in to have a hip replaced. My impression was, "Wow, what a nice old guy. He's just a little bit older than my dad would be if he was alive. I guess it's gonna be pretty quiet next door."

Wrong.

When Harold came out of the hospital with his new hip, I began to discover what the man was all about. Instead of complaining about the food in the hospital, he winked and told me how pretty his nurse was. Instead of griping about the pain, he marveled at the technology that could put a new joint in his worn-out hip. The doctors had given him a walker with tennis balls on the legs, a contraption that he was supposed to lean on for six months. He ditched it in a week and in less than a month he was out on the golf course.

And so began one of the best relationships of my life.

There is a lot to know about maintaining a little patch of lakefront, and I had every bit of it to learn. You have to know about building docks, and maintaining seawalls, and repairing yard pumps, and tying up boats, and raking seaweed, and which way the wind should be blowing before you set fire to the brush pile. You also have to know when it's time to sip a cup of coffee on the deck and watch the swans glide by, or the perfect moment to crack open the first beer on a hot Saturday afternoon.

Harold knew all these things, and he was willing to become my surrogate dad and share his knowledge with me. He had a knack of sounding incredibly gracious and offhand in gently suggesting that I might not want to hop in the water with a live power cord in my hand.

One morning, while we were sipping our coffee and watching the swans, Harold suggested that he and I become partners in buying a pontoon boat. Up to that moment I had thought that to own a pontoon boat I would have to wear polyester pants belted just under my armpits and have the phone number of my proctologist on speed dial. Wrong again.

Harold found us the perfect party barge, and we bought it at the perfect price. We spent the winter working together to restore it, he and I splitting up the work into tasks for which each of us was best suited. Harold tweaked the engine, updated the wiring, and restored the furniture on deck with beautifully handcrafted oak woodwork. I got the radio working and scraped the dried-up crud off the pontoons; I honestly don't think I've ever enjoyed myself more.

I could probably fill a book with stories about Harold. Maybe someday I will. I could talk about the time he showed me the plans, sketched on the back of an envelope, for the walnut entertainment center he was going to build that winter. About us both pretending that I had anything useful to contribute to the conversation. About watching him mill the boards he was going to use to build it, and the jaw-dropping beauty of the final piece, with its inlays and hand-carved floral work.

Or I could talk about all the little schemes he and I cooked up that didn't really work out all that well, like the time the two of us figured out a new and innovative method of installing the dock, carrying sections out over the lake, walking down the sections we had already installed. It worked too, keeping us warm, dry, and happy - for a while.

The neighbors still talk about the sight of Harold and, me standing tall, riding our half-built dock as it fell, slowly and majestically, down into the drink.

Now Harold is gone, off to the next great adventure. He was 92 years old and his health had been going downhill drastically for a while. It's been a couple of years since he could crank up his tools and produce one of his woodworking masterpieces. His amazing wife Donna had gone on ahead of him; that was another tough goodbye I had to write.

You know, it's easy at a time like this to say things like, "He had a good life," or, "At least he isn't suffering anymore," or, "He was ready." And I guess all those things would pretty much be true.

That doesn't really approach the reality of losing someone like Harold, though. For as long as I live, every time I see something I don't understand happening on the lake, or run up against something I don't know how to do, or whenever I just feel like learning a few things over a nice cold bottle of Killian's Irish Red, my first inclination will be to call Harold.

Instead, I'll just have to heave a sigh and try to figure it all out on my own. But along with that sigh I get to enjoy a little smile at the memory of the things I learned from Harold, and the things he and I learned together, and all the fun we had in the process.

Like I said, I'm a really lucky guy.

In Which I Get a Massage

Not too long ago I got my first real massage.

OK guys, go ahead and get all the stupid "Happy Ending" jokes out of your system. I'll wait. Finished? Good.

It just so happens that for my massage I went to a licensed massage therapist, a trained and highly skilled professional who has spent years studying and perfecting her craft. She is also a practicing nurse.

OK guys, get all the stupid "Naughty Nurse" jokes out of your system. I'll wait. Still waiting. Finished? Good.

The place where I booked my massage was called "Cosmic Hands..."

Really? OK, yeah, I'll wait.

As the day of my appointment approached, I have to admit that I became kind of apprehensive.

After all, my previous experience with massage was limited, and not all that great.

Back in my younger days I played a little football (I was on the team as a voluntary tackling dummy). The team employed a massage therapist whose name, I'm pretty sure, was Thor. I didn't get to see him much, since he generally worked on the more productive players – the guys who scored lots of touchdowns, the other guys who were assigned to kill and eat opposing linemen, and the constantly-injured linebacker who dated the head coach's daughter, "Crusher" (I'm guessing that this may not have actually been her real name).

The most memorable time I spent on Thor's massage table was when the big guy tried to cure a "Charlie horse" by taking my left foot and shoving the baby toe into my right ear.

During the years I spent as a competitive water skier, one of my coaches insisted that I undergo a form of massage called "Rolfing," which involved a very large woman with bionic thumbs, cast iron elbows, and a single eye in the middle of her forehead (that's the way I remember her) ripping out and rearranging all of my muscles while I shrieked and begged for either mercy or a quick death.

When I was playing "Masters," ice hockey (more often referred to as "Old Guys Who Skate

Slow And Drink Beer In The Locker Room"), I spent quite a bit of time with the chiropractor, having all my vertebrae systematically crushed and rearranged.

So when I walked through the door of Cosmic Hands I was mainly thinking that, in the interest of keeping up appearances, I should at least try to minimize the sobbing. As I stood there in the waiting room, though, I began to forget about my fear. The place was very appealing, tastefully decorated in a 60's retro kind of motif. The lights were soft, and the air was sweet with the scent of patchouli and incense. There was even one of those cool old hippie bead curtains leading back to the "business part" of the establishment.

Then, out through the bead curtains came the masseuse.

I had only spoken to her on the phone, and was mildly curious to meet her face-to-face. What I had never considered was the possibility that she might turn out to be a neighbor. I didn't know the woman all that well, but I did run into her fairly frequently in the pet food aisle at the local supermarket. So when she led me into the treatment room, smiled, and said, "I'm going to step out for a few minutes while you get undressed," I wasn't sure exactly what to do.

To put this in perspective, I'm not particularly body shy. In fact, like most men I am downright delusional about my appearance.

As a short instructional aside for the ladies, guys develop and maintain our delusions by employing a number of meticulously crafted techniques. For instance, when it comes to mirrors, we never stand in front of one and critically "take inventory" like most women seem to do. We only look at ourselves from the shoulders up, and then only at certain, carefully tested angles. That way we can wink at ourselves and say, "Looking good there, Stud," before we go off to try and find a belt that might still make it all the way around the equator and back to the buckle.

Many men also believe, despite all evidence to the contrary, that women are as anxious to feast their eyes on our naughty bits as we are to get even the most fleeting glimpse of theirs. Luckily, I have been married long enough to know way better than that. I understand that to most normal women, the sight of me in all my natural glory is more likely to be disturbing than thrilling.

What happened, as I stood there alone in that cozy little candle-lit room, listening to the relaxing sounds of soft guitar music coming from the speakers near the head of the massage table, was that I decided that I would just strip down to my boxers. That way my friend could do her job and still be able to chat with me in Aisle Six without the specter of my "winky" hanging over her head.

Figuratively speaking.

Then I came to the realization that, on that afternoon in the middle of July, under my denim shorts (the ones with the manly rivets by the pockets and the macho tool loop on the side), I was wearing my "Curious George Christmas Fun" boxer shorts. I got a mental flash of how that might play out later, in front of the Whisker Lickins. "Oh, hi," I would say. "What's new?"

"Nothing much," she would snicker. "So what did you get for Christmas from the Man in the Yellow Hat?"

So standing there next to the massage table, I had a decision to make. Do I 'fess up and just let her see the boxers? Do I abandon all modesty, strip down to nothing, hide George, and risk the whole winky-specter thing? Or do I stay fully dressed and wind up coming across like some deeply religious congressman on one of those rare evenings when he is not out trolling for gay sex in an airport men's room?

I decided to stick with Curious George and hope for the best.

The masseuse was way cooler and more professional than I expected. She had a pretty good laugh, made a sort of call-back joke about Monkey

Chow, then said, "OK, Funny Guy, lose 'em. I've seen you walk, and I think we need to do a little work on loosening up those glutes."

If you don't know what "glutes" are, I'll wait while you take it to Google, then get all the stupid jokes out of your system. Finished? Good.

It turns out that the massage itself was really pleasant and deeply relaxing, with hardly any whimpering on my part. I can testify that by the time she was finished with me my glutes were totally loose, and all my fretting about "Curious George Christmas Fun" was for nothing.

I'm just glad we didn't have to deal with the pictures of the muscular guy in a loin cloth on the "He-Man, Masters of the Universe" boxers I was originally going to wear...

A Miracle?

Since late last week anyone more alert than, say, a block of wood, has been obsessing on the dramatic story of US Airways Flight 1549. For any of my readers who actually happen to be blocks of wood, this was the commercial airline flight that sucked some extremely surprised Canada geese into both engines and lost power 3000 feet over New York City.

The pilot of the airplane, Captain Chesley B. Sullenberger III (for reasons that should be fairly obvious, everyone calls him "Sully"), made a series of split-second decisions, flew dead-stick across Midtown, barely cleared the George Washington Bridge, and executed a masterful crash landing in the middle of the Hudson river. All 150 passengers and crew aboard walked away from Flight 1549 without serious injury.

Almost immediately I found myself a little bit uncomfortable that this story has been labeled "The Miracle on the Hudson," although it took me a while to figure out why. The story was a lot of things – wonderful, heart-warming, spectacular, amazing, even life-affirming. And certainly very fortunate. But one thing it was not was a "miracle."

You see, to me a miracle is something like magic, where the thing that happens is outside the laws of nature. Turning water into wine, parting the sea, or the Tigers actually polishing off a World Series – those are miracles.

What we really saw on board Flight 1549 was not a miracle - it was a sublime example of a team of really talented people, led by a highly skilled Captain, all thoroughly trained to do the jobs they were expected to do. We saw a pilot and crew make use of every sliver of skill, knowledge and good luck they could find to work toward the best possible outcome.

And then there were the ferry and water taxi captains – those Magellans of the Manhattan waterways, who are sometimes given about the same respect as the tattooed and toothless guys who run the tilt-a-whirl at the county fair.

Ferry Captain Vince Lombardi, heading out for Hoboken, was startled to see the A320 in the river with 150 people standing on the wings, floating down toward Battery Park. He reacted instantly, ordering his crew to implement their practiced "man overboard drill," and charged to the rescue. It is arguable that 150 people made it home for dinner because of Captain Lombardi and his colleagues.

So what we really saw was the result of careful and systematic preparation; ditching and evacuation plans on the plane, rescue procedures on the ferries and water taxis, and thorough water disaster training by the fire department. And we saw competent professionals making the best use of all that preparation, doing exactly what they had been trained to do.

This is not to suggest that Captain Sully, or his crew, or the captains and crews of the ferries and water taxis - or even the passengers of Flight 1549, who shrugged off panic and helped each other to safety - are not all heroes. They are, in every possible sense of the word. In fact, it seems like calling their experience a miracle actually detracts from their heroism. If there was a divine hand in the outcome of Flight 1549, it was seen in putting all those incredible people right where they were.

There is a word that comes to mind here, a word that has been frequently misused for the past few years. We hear it hurled as a pejorative at climate scientists, economic scholars, or any of our nation's political leaders who try to persuade from a position of knowledge and reason rather than intolerance and fear. They sneer at anyone with advanced education, training and experience who resorts to timely and skillful interpretation of the facts to guide and support their actions.

The word I'm thinking of is, "elite." Folks who call others "elite" as an insult are apparently not aware that the word actually means, "the very best; better trained or more talented."

With that in mind, it seems like it might be a good idea to pay attention to all those "elite" climate scientists who have accurately predicted the super-storms, floods, droughts and other manifestations of decades of dumping thousands of tons of pollutants into our atmosphere; or the "elite" economists who can help guide us out of the financial devastation unleashed by the fiscal insanity of the Bush years; or that "elite" President Obama, who has somehow managed to fly our country toward economic and actual safety with all the engines continuously sabotaged by his political opponents.

In any case, it sure seems like there are 150 people, along with all their families and all their friends, who are pretty thankful that Flight 1549 was in the hands of that "elite" Captain Sully.

My Latest Girl Car

In this column I have talked from time to time about "guy cars" and "girl cars." I have pointed out that there are a few fundamental differences in how most men and women view their automobiles.

The typical guy wants a car that is an expression of dominance over his personal universe. He wants it to project an image of his status and virility to the world. He wants it to be a four-wheeled extension of his ideal self, looking and sounding as powerful and in-charge as he (comically) imagines himself to be.

Most women are happy with a car if the engine starts when you turn the key.

Of course, there are other features a woman will appreciate in a car, like seat heaters, or a color scheme that looks good with her eyes. But mostly, women take a pretty practical approach to personal transportation; they would like to be able to travel to a desired destination in reasonable style and comfort, and they would like to have enough room in the vehicle to take all their crap along with them.

Young women tend to drive small cars, because they themselves are small and they apparently don't have all that much crap. Still, their colorful little Fiestas and Civics can be expected to contain a fairly comprehensive selection of music, designer sunglasses, reading material, snack foods, cosmetics, and at least a basic wardrobe (especially shoes), because, well, you never really know, do you?

Once a woman has a family, this whole dynamic sort of explodes. She not only needs space for all her crap, but also for her kids and their crap. And, as every parent is well aware, kids can generate an awful lot of crap! So, in the latter part of the twentieth century, this need for additional crap capacity led to the creation of the ultimate "girl car," the Minivan.

The Minivan can best be described as a sort of gigantic rolling handbag, with room for at least half a soccer team - complete with appropriate equipment, costumes and snack foods. And it is designed to go just fast enough to avoid being classified as a geological formation.

I bring all this up because I am now the driver of a Minivan.

As I have pointed out before, I have always driven "girl cars." I know this because within a week of buying every car I've ever owned, all my male friends start telling me how they just bought the same car for their wives. Or their daughters. Or that they had been considering getting their daughters the same model I bought, but decided on the bigger engine than mine has.

And then all my female friends start telling me they think that my car is "really cute." Trust me on this ladies, "really cute" is not what any man wants to hear about the image of his status and virility.

Now I won't go into a lot of detail about how I wound up with a Minivan. What I have been telling everybody is that I put up with it because it was an opportunity to get a lot of vehicle for the money, and that it is ideal for hauling my guitars and other gear around to gigs.

Note the use of the word "hauling" to make the whole thing sound manly and industrial.

But the simple truth is, I like the Minivan, and I'm not entirely certain why. Sure, it is practical - and everyone who knows me knows that "Practical" is my middle name. (That last sentence, by the way, is an example of "irony," sort of like

Sarah Palin complaining on Fox News about not-always-truthful journalism. My middle name is not really "Practical.")

I think the thing I actually like best about driving a Minivan is that nobody expects me to compete with other guys in that whole "dominance over the personal universe" thing. I'm talking about when you're sitting at a stop light, and the guy next to you races his engine and smirks at you as if to say, "Come on, Daffodil, let's see what you got," so you race your engine right back at him, and then one thing leads to another, and the next thing you know you're trying to explain to your wife how you wound up somewhere in Iowa with a broken transmission and a speeding ticket.

We've all been there, right guys?

Instead, as a driver of a Minivan, I can now just smile, shrug, and when the light changes drift happily - if a bit tectonically - on down the street.

Please, No More Tiger Tales!

Last weekend I spent more time watching the Masters golf tournament on television than I like to admit. I guess I find it strangely comforting to see tanned, handsome, self-assured millionaire touring golf professionals occasionally shank a five iron into a sand trap.

To me the highlight of the weekend was Fred Couples making a serious run for the Green Jacket. I loved this because:

a) He is fifty years old and has more gray hair than I do;

b) His name is "Fred;"

c) In an elite sport where everything a player uses, wears, eats, drinks, or thinks about is computer engineered for maximum performance and endorsement value, this guy was playing the most prestigious tournament in professional golf wearing slip-on boat shoes with no socks.

Also, I found it mildly interesting to see Tiger Woods making his comeback after five months away from competitive golf.

Now, I shouldn't have to recap the shenanigans that have kept Tiger's putter on ice for all that time. Since his wife capped off last year's Thanksgiving weekend by chipping Tiger out of his Escalade with a sand wedge, we have enjoyed non-stop media coverage.

We have seen hospital reports, police reports, some really world-class Mea Culpa press conferences, and more salacious photographs of waitresses with surgically enhanced body parts than you'll find in an issue of Truck Stop Hooters magazine.

We were even subjected to possibly the most bizarre television moment I have ever witnessed, a Nike ad in which a sober-faced Tiger stares at the camera for thirty seconds while the recorded voice of his deceased father, Earl Woods, chews him out; "... I want to know what your thinking was..."

So here's the deal; I watched Tiger at the Masters because I wanted to see how his short game held up to the layoff.

I do not care what his thinking was.

In fact, I just plain don't want to know who Tiger sleeps with. Whether he hits the sack with a skanky porn star or the Swedish supermodel (with

sand wedge) he has at home on an eight-figure re-
tainer, it makes exactly zero difference in my life.

I REALLY DON'T CARE!

I do kind of feel sorry for his children, as
much as you can feel sorry for somebody who
stands to someday inherit a big chunk of a nearly
billion-dollar estate. But they are not the first kids
who ever had to cope with the idea that their superstar dad can be a total moron when it comes to
big hair and cleavage. Odds are, they'll be all right.

And don't bother to write and tell me that Tiger has failed to live up to his solemn obligation as
a role model for the Youth of America. If your kid
is a golfer, then he or she should admire Tiger's
golf swing and focus under pressure. In those areas
he is one of the best who ever strolled down a fair-
way at Augusta.

But frankly, if your children are getting their
moral guidance from a guy who makes his living
hitting a ball with a stick, I have to say right at the
get-go that you are pretty much falling short in
your job as a parent.

This goes for any sports hero. I think we can
all admire and emulate how they throw a football,
shoot a puck, hit three-pointers, or crank base-
balls into the left field upper deck (unless they
have been cheating to do it - I'm talking to you,
Mark McGwire).

But if our heroes break laws, it's an issue between them and the law. And if they mess things up with their families, as far as I'm concerned that is an issue between them and their families.

Tiger Woods has always seemed like a generally decent sort of guy, soft-spoken and polite. Maybe this is why we were all so surprised to find out just how much of a world-class moron he was when it came to big hair and cleavage.

But you know what? I'm over that now. Oh sure, I hope Tiger can get things all regrouped in his personal life and the Woods family can live happily ever after. If not, oh well.

And if Tiger or Elin or the kids ever need any help or advice from me, they can feel free to call and I'll be happy to give it to them. Otherwise, I really don't want to hear any more about it.

Caelyn

My new granddaughter was born last night.

Now, a lot of things can happen to you that are really great; finding a $20 bill in the pocket of a jacket you haven't worn in a couple of years; your $1 lotto ticket hitting for $100; the Detroit Red Wings winning the Stanley Cup (OK, so not this year); pulling off the road with a groan when the police cruiser lights go on, only to watch him speed right past you to haul down that jerk in the black Escalade who cut you off a couple of miles back; Snickers bars.

But a few events come along in a lifetime that stand so far above all that other stuff that they make the coolest fireworks display that ever rumbled your chest and made your heart pound seem like a complete waste of time. Having a grandchild is one of those events.

My son emailed me a picture of himself sitting on the bed, looking down at his minutes-old daughter, who was lying on his lap all swaddled in pink and looking right back up at the biggest, most important man she will ever know. I smiled when I saw it and typed a reply to him:

"OK Son, NOW you understand!"

You see, like most parents, I have tried to explain parenthood to him almost since that day, just a little over thirty years ago, when I sat staring in amazement at my minute-s old Patrick lying in my lap. I tried to describe the overwhelming familiarity you feel the first time you lay eyes on that red, wrinkled little creature, your absolute joy in his first big juicy belch, and why you don't really get mad when you pull off his diaper in a careless moment and take a fountain of pee right between the eyes.

I tried to make him comprehend why I was so completely delighted the day we discovered that he had grown taller than me. Or why I cried when I gave his little bike away to the church rummage sale. Or how each time I found myself unable to give him something that he really, really, REALLY wanted, I felt like a miserable, despicable failure.

For all those years he listened to what I said, and he believed me, and he thought he understood exactly what I was trying to tell him. He apparently took my word for the general concept, because, helped along by the love of his beautiful wife and, I assume, by basic biology, he went ahead and decided to start his own family.

But at 9:09 PM on Friday, April 20, 2012, the meaning of all those things became truly clear to my son, in a moment all mothers and fathers know but that words can only attempt describe. At that instant I was able to welcome him into the huge and happy (mostly) Club of Parents.

Of course, also at that instant my wife and I became, by official decree of the new parents, "Nana" and "PopPop," which might just be the coolest thing we've ever been called. I sure hope the kid decides to go with the flow on this.

The emotional impact of becoming PopPop has been slightly less surprising than my Daddy moment was all those years ago, but no less intense. There is the same overwhelming sense of love, and awe, and wonder, and frank disbelief that anyone or anything so beautiful could exist.

In a lot of ways, this grandparent gig is even better than parenthood. It is certainly more fun. Neither my wife or I had to participate in the delivery, other than to show up afterward, listen sympathetically to all the details, and make comments like, "Yeah, I remember that," and, "Oh God, I really remember that!"

As PopPop, I can simply gaze in loving wonder at my granddaughter's perfect little baby mouth and not have to worry about how I'm going to pay for her braces. If her diaper suddenly inflates, I can just smile, shrug, and hand her over.

My son never had an chance to get to know my wife's parents very well, or to know mine at all. He grew up mostly without grandparents, and I feel like that was a real loss. Caelyn is lucky enough to have a full set of grandmas and grandpas, and all four of us are conspiring to spoil her shamelessly.

So I take it as a matter of personal responsibility to do everything in my power to let my darling little Caelyn (and, with any luck, a whole mess of brothers and sisters down the road) know how much fun it can be to have a PopPop. I intend to at least help introduce her to the wonders of picture books, tambourines, happy books, water skis, bubble gum, sad books, drums, Pixar movies, marbles, ukuleles, poetry books, harmonicas, ice skates, Elephant Ears, finger paints, hockey sticks, and Snickers bars.

In fact, when the time comes, and in the spirit of exacting retribution on my son for every naughty thing he ever did while he was growing up, PopPop might just teach little Caelyn how to play the banjo.

Banjo Picker Blues

My name is Mike, and I'm a banjo picker.

In my last column I suggested that I intend to exact a particularly fiendish sort of retribution on my son by teaching my beautiful new granddaughter how to play the banjo, just like her "PopPop" does. This is not an idle threat. To a lot of people (most people), turning their child into a banjo player would be considered just slightly worse than helping her start a skunk ranch in the back yard to raise money toward buying her very own Jolly Junior Seal Team Explosives Kit.

What I'm saying here is that banjos are very possibly not the most beloved of all the world's musical instruments.

For one thing, they are not seen as being particularly sophisticated. Ever since 1972, when the movie Deliverance forever linked bluegrass music with the squealing of pig-like creatures, the distant sound of a banjo echoing down the river has made canoeists everywhere paddle faster.

Banjos are also, admittedly, very loud. In fact, volume is generally considered one of the important attributes of a good instrument. I have a sort of medium-quality "resonator" banjo, meaning that it is only loud enough to deafen a jackhammer operator at 100 yards. A really good Gibson resonator can actually blister paint. I wish I had me one of them there ones...

There are thousands of banjo jokes around:

There's nothing I like better than the sound of a banjo - unless it's the sound of a moose giving birth to a Toyota.

or:

Q: You're locked in a room with a tiger, a rattlesnake and a banjo player. You have a gun, but only two bullets. What do you do?

A: Shoot the banjo player. Twice.

or:

A guy walks into a bar with a 14 foot gator on a chain and asks the bartender, "Do you serve banjo players here?"

The bartender says "Yeah, sure mister."

The guy says "OK, I'll have a beer. And bring us a couple of banjo players for my gator."

I think these jokes are all cruel and more than a little bit offensive, so I won't dignify them by repeating them. Except, of course for the ones I just did repeat. And these:

Q: What are the seven toughest years in a banjo player's life?

A: Second grade.

The Sheriff pulls a banjo player over, walks up to his car window and asks him, "Got any ID?" The banjo player says, "'Bout what?"

A banjo is a lot better than a harmonica. It's just too hard to beat a banjo player with a harmonica.

You know how serious musicians define perfect pitch? It's the sound a banjo makes when it's tossed into a dumpster, bounces off an accordion and smashes a mandolin.

You get the idea. Of course, that last one takes a pretty good swipe at accordions and mandolins - which we also feature in the band, Dr. Mike & The Sea Monkeys, from time to time.

My wife is so anti-banjo that I am not allowed to play it when she is in the same house. In fact, I'm smart if I lay off whenever she's in the same county. The only thing she says if I get the banjo out when she is around is, "Why don't you play out in the shed."

If anyone knows the lyrics and chords to "Out In The Shed," email them to me and I'll learn it for her.

What really brought all this to mind is that not too long ago an eighty-eight year-old man named Earl Scruggs passed away. For those of you who side with the guy in the bar with the gator, and so might not be all that well-schooled in banjo lore, Earl is generally considered the patron saint of the bluegrass banjo, having virtually invented the most popular style of playing it. There are other fine approaches to banjo picking, but "Scruggs Style" is what most people are familiar with - just think of the "Theme From the Beverly Hillbillies."

Most of us who pick banjos have mixed feelings about Mr. Scruggs. On one hand, hearing him play almost certainly explains why we play in the first place. I even had the opportunity to see him in person, maybe 25 years ago, and I'm still trying to catch my breath.

On the other hand, people who play for money, especially those of us who don't play the banjo as a primary instrument, usually make a lot of compromises - like rewriting songs to skip chords we don't know how to play. When you do that, you can count on a parlor player who has spent years getting Foggy Mountain Breakdown

down note-for-note coming up to you with helpful advice like, "That ain't the way Earl done it."

But I guess that's not Earl's fault. In fact, based on everything I've heard and read about the amazing Earl Scruggs, I feel pretty confident that he would be likely to say something more like, "Well now son, what you did there was interesting. Why don't you try..."

So overall, while the toughest seven years of my life were indeed second grade, the banjo is just plain fun. And I guess I'm proud of my picking, such as it is, so I ain't likely to stop any time soon.

Caely Honey, does PopPop ever have a treat for you!

The Fine Art of Delivering Phone Books

My new phone book arrived the other day, delivered directly into the bushes by the front door. It was in a plastic bag, but it was jammed in crooked and the twist tie was not properly attached. I was appalled! As a trained professional, it was almost painful to witness such shoddy work.

You see, at one (brief) point in my (not so brief) working life I was myself a phone book delivery guy. Of course, it's been something like thirty-five years since I served on the front lines of the Battle For Handy And Reliable Home and Business Directory Information, and maybe the standards have fallen since then.

I joined the proud ranks of phone book deliverers during one of several times in my life when I was a little on the light side of completely broke, and I wanted to buy a birthday present for my wife. When I read the Help Wanted ad in the newspaper that said I could earn as much as three dollars an hour if I was a reliable self-starter, I literally dove for the phone.

The first thing I had to do was fill out an application, which made me a little bit nervous. I mean, what if I failed to measure up to the high standards of the service fraternity I was trying to join? Fortunately, the toughest questions on the form were, "Do you have your own car?" and, "Have you ever served time in a Federal prison?" Apparently the State pen would be just fine.

Before long I received a letter telling me that my application had been accepted (the answers were "yes" and "no," respectively), and that I was to show up at an Orientation Meeting in a small conference room at the Holiday Inn. It would be a sort of basic training program for me and a group of my fellow hopefuls, an opportunity to learn the finer points of the trade.

The first thing we did was watch a short film, with a title something like, "So You Want to Deliver Phone Books." It dealt with our vital role in the telecommunications industry, and our solemn obligation to each and every one of the citizens on our routes.

It turns out we were expected to knock on every door and personally hand the phone book to the recipient. If nobody was home, we were to leave a note on the door and try again later. After three attempts, we were instructed to carefully bag the book and leave it inside the storm door.

For each book delivered this way, we were to be paid eleven cents.

The film also provided us with a list of dramatically illustrated "Do's and Don'ts." The most memorable vignette involved a woman actor wearing a housecoat and hair curlers, opening the door to a clean-cut and innocent young Deliverer, standing on the porch with a fresh new phone book in hand.

When our sultry domestic siren made a transparent (and fairly nauseating) attempt to lure the young professional into her lair, potentially diverting him from his sacred duty to his appointed rounds, he firmly and politely refused, handed her the book with a confident smile, and strode off into the sunset.

After the film, I took a good look around at my fellow Knights of the Phone Book. Hoping to make a good impression on my new employers, I had come to our training session wearing a sport coat and tie. I was a little out of sync with my colleagues on that point, since the accepted uniform leaned more toward cutoff jeans, white "wife beater" tank tops, and tattoos.

The wife beaters made it easy to determine that I was also the only one there who did not have at least one tattoo.

The next step was picking our routes. Each route consisted of about 200 addresses, and so was worth about $22. The official advice for all the new deliverers was to take one or maybe two routes, just to get the hang of it. Then, if everything went well, we could always came back for more.

Always rational and cautious, I went ahead and signed up for ten routes.

Next week, The Bearer Of The Books

The Fine Art of
Delivering Phone Books
Part II - The Bearer of the Books

Last week I started to tell you about the time I decided to join the Few, the Proud, the Phone Book Deliverers. I had passed the initial rigorous screening (I could prove that I had a pulse and was not on probation) and I had clawed my way through nearly twenty minutes of arduous training. Now I was ready to take to the streets.

I have always been ambitious, and I was more than a little bit broke, so I had signed up for ten routes. At two hundred addresses per route and eleven cents per successfully delivered book, this meant that after just ringing a few door bells and saying, "Madam, I hold in my hands a brand new phone book, yours to enjoy with my compliments," I stood to bring home a cool $220!

When I picked up my route sheets, I began to sense that there were a few aspects of this whole project that I had not really bothered to calculate. For one thing, the sheaf of names, all sorted by street address, contained around two thousand addresses, and added up to something like seventy pages.

That's a lot of door bells.

And then there were the books themselves. At a little more than a pound per book, my two thousand books weighed well over a ton. It took six spring-crushing trips in my 1968 Volkswagen microbus to get them all home.

Nevertheless, I set out the next day with a set of route sheets, a trusty old VW creaking under the weight of phone books, and high hopes.

The first problem cropped up at my first stop, when an elderly woman came to the door but refused to open it. I could hear her muffled shouting; "What do you want?"

"Madam," I shouted back, "I hold in my hands a brand new phone book, yours to enjoy..."

"What?"

"I said, 'I hold in my hands...'"

"What?"

"Phone book. I have your new phone book!"

"What?"

"Maybe if you open the door..."

"I can't hear you with the door closed! Now, go away!"

"But I'm supposed to give it to you in person!"

"Go away!"

I put her book in a plastic bag with "Let Your Fingers Do The Walking" elegantly silkscreened on the outside, shouted "Thank you!" and moved on.

Except for the woman who wanted me to come in and take a look at her garbage disposal and the man who came to the door wearing a scarlet leotard (he thought I would probably be interested in seeing his collection of Hummel figurines) this was pretty much the reception I got at the next twenty houses.

The second problem I had was that I couldn't very easily carry more than about five books at a time without having some of them sail unceremoniously into the bushes, so I was making a lot of trips back and forth to the van. By mid-afternoon I had delivered about thirty books and I was exhausted, so I went home to rest, think, and enjoy a brain food lunch (a peanut butter sandwich and a beer).

When I passed a Kroger parking lot on the way back to my route that afternoon, the brain food kicked in and I solved the problem of how to tote all those books. It seems that you can easily get about 20 or 30 phone books in a shopping cart, and if you don't steal one with a screwed-up wheel it will roll up and down the street just fine.

And so for the next three weeks I rattled from house to house, diligently updating each occupant's access to the latest business and residential contact data. I filled out my seventy pages of paperwork, turned it in, and ultimately picked up a paycheck big enough to buy my wife's birthday present. I even had enough left over to buy the parts to repair the van's suspension.

And yes, I did return that cart to the Kroger parking lot.

What's the worst job you've ever had? Send an email to mike@learnedsofar.com, and tell me all about it.

Rabbit Hunting:
Rabbits 1, Hunters 0

I might be the only male resident of Michigan who is not spending these early days of November stockpiling ammunition and Slim Jims in anticipation of deer season. It's not that I object to hunting; I just don't care to do it. And I don't have anything bad to say about hunters. Of course, this is partly because I make it a rule never to say anything bad about people with guns.

I think most of my reluctance to blast woodland creatures goes back to when I was about twelve years old and my dad, also not a hunter, decided to take me out to shoot some rabbits. Two things made him decide to do this:

1) He had inherited a single-shot 12-gauge shotgun from his grandfather, who had told him that it was good for rabbit hunting.

2) He believed that we could probably figure out what to do with some dead rabbits if we happened to come home with any.

So one bright Saturday morning my dad handed me a burlap bag for "the kill" and a small red box of shotgun shells, A.K.A., "the bullets." Then he piled me, the shotgun, and our dog, a plump little brown female mutt named Scamp, into his white Volkswagen Beetle and we headed out. Scamp kept watch with her head out the window, alertly smashing bugs with her nose and forehead.

We were going to hunt on land belonging to a man my dad knew, a place reportedly so rich in rabbits that, "...you can't throw a stick without hitting one." We were bringing Scamp along to "flush" rabbits, and the gun just in case we couldn't find any sticks to throw.

It had not occurred to my dad that most hunting dogs receive some sort of training, and that Scamp might not have any idea how to "flush" anything more cunning than a French fry. As soon as we opened the car door, the dog bolted out and vanished into the waist-deep weeds. We stood there expectantly waiting for her to reappear. Nothing. Not a whisper of movement. Not a bark. Nothing.

"Maybe she had a heart attack," I said. "She is getting kind of old."

"She's sneaking up on them," my dad replied authoritatively. "She'll be flushing them any second." Then a look of panic came over his face. "Hey, there's no bullets in the gun! Quick, get me a bullet!"

I sprinted back to the car on my quest for ammunition, but when I got there I sort of tripped on the door frame. This catapulted me across the passenger seat and my hand hit the box of shells I had left on the dash, launching it in an arcing trajectory onto the floor, so that the lid popped open and the shells scattered under the driver's seat. As I flopped around the car fishing for ammunition, my dad provided words of encouragement;

"I gave you the bullets and said 'hang onto the bullets' didn't I? I don't remember telling you to dump the bullets under the seat. Do you remember me telling you to dump the bullets under the seat? Now we're going to be up to our butts in rabbits and all the bullets are under the seat..."

He froze at the sound of violent rustling in the weeds, a sound that might be made by hundreds of rabbits being "flushed" by a fat little brown dog. At the same moment my hand closed around a shell. "Here you go," I shouted, lobbing it in his direction. The shell sailed past his ear and into the weeds.

"Ok, I missed that one," he said. "Next time you find a bullet, hand it to me."

I located another shell under the floor mat, ran over and slapped it into his hand. He cracked the barrel of the gun, rammed the shell in place, snapped the barrel shut, aimed and fired.

You know, a 12-gauge shotgun is a lot louder than you might think. My father was a large man, and physically strong, but the combination of recoil and surprise knocked him off his feet and onto the seat of his pants. As for me, I just threw my hands over my head and fell heroically to the ground. After a few stunned seconds my father said, "Are you shot?"

"No. How about you?"

"Not as far as I can tell."

We got up and looked in the direction he had been aiming, to see a sort of crater torn into the weeds. We walked tentatively toward it, expecting, I suppose, to find a bunch of little rabbit pot roasts all bundled up and ready to cook. Instead, we found Scamp lying in the weeds.

"Oh my God, I shot the dog," my dad said.

"I don't think so," I said. "There's not a scratch on her." We discussed my earlier heart attack theory for awhile, and were wondering just how much dog we could jam into a burlap body bag, when she seemed to revive. She was pretty annoyed, but in perfect health.

After a lot of debate on the way home, we decided that all the noise was just the dog prancing through the weeds, and that she had simply fainted when the load of buckshot whistled over her head.

Scamp went on to live a long and increasingly corpulent life, never again stalking anything larger than a cricket and spending thunderstorms and all holidays involving fireworks hunkered down under a bed.

The "bullets" were all eventually recovered from the Volkswagen, and they now sit, more than thirty years later, safely back in their red box on a shelf in my basement. I'm not real sure where the shotgun is.

And the rabbits of the world are safe - at least from me.

Scooby-Doo, I Facebook You

Facebook is fantastic. It gives us an unprecedented opportunity to appear in public in our underwear. Unfortunately, for most of us this turns out to be brightly colored Scooby-Doo boxer shorts.

I mean that metaphorically, of course.

One Sunday evening not too long ago I came across a Facebook post by an old friend. He said: "Started watching the Super Bowl while eating supper, and am still waiting for a truly creative commercial."

This woke me right up. Here I was, chowing Twizzlers and finding out (with detailed photographic evidence) whose grandkids had spent the day making snowballs, and at that moment I was supposed to be at a Super Bowl party, chowing hot wings, watching the most important sporting event of the century, and finding out if we were going to be treated to a Halftime Wardrobe Mal-function with somebody more interesting than Janet Jackson.

I hate missing out on hot wings.

Fighting off a surge of panic, I looked below my friend's post at the comments from some of his other friends. The gist of what they were all saying was, "The Super Bowl is next week ... you're watching the Pro Bowl."

What a relief!

Ironically, my friend with the sketchy knowl-edge of the NFL Postseason is also one of the wisest, most intelligent people I know. He taught science at the middle school in our little town and retired after many years of being that one really special teacher who changes the lives of countless kids.

In his defense, there is no disgrace in totally not giving a crap about the most important sport-ing event of the century. Other than the possibil-ity of missing out on those hot wings, and maybe a truly creative commercial or two, I totally don't give a crap either.

What is interesting is that our modern infor-mation age makes it possible for us to share every one of our brain farts – our Scooby-Doo boxers – in real time, with everyone we know.

Let's say you do something really stupid. Let's say you unscrew the cap on the bottle of dried habanero pepper flakes instead of using the flip-up thing that covers the shaker holes, then dump the whole 6 oz. bottle of slow, painful death on top of your slice of pizza. In the old days, your buddy would call you an idiot, you would agree, then you would scrape off as much pepper as possible and wash down that slice with a 12-pack of beer. Maybe two.

These days you and your buddy are honor-bound to document the incident for social media posterity. You snap some iPhone shots of the mound of habaneros. You go to video mode and shoot establishing shots of your face and your buddy's face, expressing surprise. You shoot some B-roll footage of the pizza box, the beer, and for no real reason, your buddy's cat over on the couch licking his nether parts.

Then your buddy films you taking your first bite. Since this is now a full-on multimedia project, you don't scrape the habaneros off the slice; you just go for it. He catches the way your eyes bug out, and the way you break into an immediate dripping sweat, and the cyanotic blue glow of your cheeks. He documents your desperate grab for the beer. He does a slow circular pan around the EMTs as they perform their resuscitation attempts.

Once the film has been edited and uploaded to your timeline, along with a concurrent Twitter post and Tumblr update, the fun really starts. The first fifteen or twenty comments are all along the lines of, "What's that stuff?" and, "One time I spilled a bunch of cinnamon too! LOL! LOL! LOL! LOL!" and, "Did you get my text about switching shifts next Saturday?"

After you wade into the comment stream to let everybody know that "them ain't no cinnamon flakes," you begin to get the more poignant comments like, "Dummy!" and "Geeze, you doof!" and, "What's the MATTER with you?"

Before long, one of your Christian friends somehow locates a Psalm that deals with this very situation; "Eat thou not the pepperonis of perdition lest ye be consumed in the eternal flames of habanero..." Helen Helpful, who apparently believes that everything she sees on Facebook is occurring live suggests, "Quick, eat 4 tablespoons of mayonnaise and drink some pickle juice. But not the sweet kind."

An environmentally-oriented friend posts, "Now, that's what I call global warming ;-D" Then a troll comes along with, "Oh, right, blamm it on globul worming. Ur a moran!"

Then people start sharing your post on their own timelines. In less than an hour you have a minor Facebook sensation on your hands, with 1,596 comments and more than 2,500 "likes." You are the newest Social Media Celebrity!

And the profit you earn for burning out your esophagus on camera is:

Nothing. Zip. Zilch. Nada. Bupkis. A couple of thousand close friends, most of whom you have never met, have had a chance to check out your Scooby-Doo boxers, and the only thing you have to show for it is that everything you eat is going to taste like habaneros for a couple of months. Plus, while the EMTs were working on you, you missed the Super Bowl.

It's a brave new world.

No Requiem For Red Wings

The Detroit Red Wings did not win the Stanley Cup this year. Yikes! Our Wings are the most magnificent sports franchise since Ogg's Cave Clubbers dominated the old Neanderthal Leagues and won twenty-one straight Pleistocene Cups. How could they possibly have lost?

For those of you who do not live in Michigan, or for those of you who do live in Michigan and who are not Detroit Red Wings fanatics (we know who both of you are and where you live...), I should give you a little background.

In ice hockey, the highest achievement possible is winning the Stanley Cup. This is a trophy named after a nineteenth century British Governor of Canada, Lord Stanley of Preston, Earl of Derby and Count of Crosschecking. After watching an impressive hockey contest back in 1893, Lord Stanley apparently figured that the players must be pretty darned proud of their accomplishments, and really thirsty, so he bought them a big silver cup to carve their names on and drink Molson out of.

The best hockey teams in North America have been doing that ever since.

To win the Stanley Cup an NHL team has to survive four best-of-seven playoff rounds against other teams who were good enough in the regular season to make it into the playoffs. This means playing anywhere between sixteen and twenty-eight high stakes hockey games in a little less than three months against skilled and highly motivated teams.

In other words, getting through the NHL Playoffs is kind of like fighting a small war, only it involves a lot more bloodshed.

The Detroit Red Wings have been around almost as long as the Cup has, and they have a long history of success. They won the Stanley Cup last year, their fourth since 1997, after racking up the best record in the NHL during the 82 games of the regular season. For the past fifteen years, they have been considered one of the most powerful hockey teams in history.

They are also only - unlike Ogg's guys, who really have to be considered more of an evolutionary side track - human. This year in the Finals they came up against the Pittsburgh Penguins, the team

they defeated last year to win the Stanley Cup.
Even though they went into the finals with many
of their best players injured, the Wings were still
favored to win without too much trouble. The
Penguin's coach was in his first season as an NHL
head coach, and while the Penguins key talent
were all healthy, most of them had trouble growing
decent beards. How could the Red Wings lose?

But they did. They played as well and as hard
as they were able to play, and the Penguins were
able to play harder and better. The Wings' mental
toughness and experience could not overcome all
the torn hamstrings and pulled groins. Red Wings
captain Nicklas Lidstrom played in the finals less
than a week after undergoing testicular surgery
to repair damage from being speared right in the
naughty bits by Patrick Sharp during the Chicago
series. The spirit may be willing, but geeze!

So in the end, the Red Wings simply wore
out, and now the Penguins will get to spend the
summer taking turns drinking beer out of Lord
Stanley's Cup, the one with their names freshly
carved into the side of it. They played hard, they
played well and they earned it.

But there is also an image from that night that
no real hockey fan will ever forget. After the game
Nicklas Lidstrom stood at center ice leaning on
his stick, politely waiting for the Penguins' captain
to shake his hand.

It's a small thing, but the handshake after a hard-fought series is considered an important part of the chivalry of the game. Every other Penguin had taken a short break from the manic celebration that will dominate their lives for the next three months to recognize their opponents.

The Penguins' captain is a breathtakingly immature scoring machine named Sidney Crosby, who is famous for devoting more energy during important games to whining and baiting referees than he does to exercising his considerable talent.

While his teammates were showing respect for the Red Wings and for the game, Crosby was too busy dancing with the Penguins' equipment manager to shake hands with a man who is universally acknowledged to be one of the greatest hockey players ever to set foot on the ice. After an embarrassing wait, Lidstrom gave up and quietly skated away.

So the Penguins won the NHL's annual War of Attrition and claimed the Stanley Cup. With the exception of their captain, those young men deserve to be respected as the champions they are.

And so do our Detroit Red Wings. Is there anybody else around here who will have trouble waiting till next season?

In Which I Discover the Senior Menu at Denny's

OK, it has finally happened; I ordered a meal from the "Senior" Menu at Denny's.

I know, right?

Since my sixtieth birthday earlier this year, I gave up my ski boat to spend more time on the pontoon boat. Then I started driving a minivan. Next thing you know I'll be pulling my pants up under my armpits and wearing socks to church.

I know, right?

For those of you who have not yet heard their family doctor say, "Wow, you really remind me of my grandfather - only older," you'll find Denny's Coot Cuisine on the back page, just below a Kid's menu that features highly nutritious choices for those precious little growing bodies - like a heaping bowl of goldfish crackers.

I have to admit it, they do offer a pretty good selection of Geezer Chow. If your wife is sitting across the table and giving you The Stare, you can go the healthy route and order an egg white omelet, a cup of fruit, and a bowl of oatmeal. There are more than 8 grams of fiber in that meal, though, so the odds are pretty good you'll be enjoying at least some your new-found health staring at a phone number and what is apparently intended to be a pair of breasts drawn in Sharpie on the door to the second stall in the men's room.

If you're not downwind of The Stare, you can go all daredevil and enjoy Country Fried Steak with a side of bacon, smothered with sausage gravy. If your heart actually explodes in the booth, Denny's will be happy to give a two-for-one coupon to your next of kin.

The first thing I noticed about the stuff on the Wrinkle Ranch Roundup is that the portions are smaller. This is presumably because us Wrinkle Ranchers don't get all that hungry, now that we no longer move any faster than a glacier or a Department of Motor Vehicles worker. On the other hand, it may just be that they figure we won't have the strength to carry a doggie bag out to the car.

The other significant thing about the Dodder Fodder is the prices, which seem to acknowledge the idea that most of us older folks are not totally up to speed with a world in which we pay $2.50 for a candy bar or more than $4 per gallon for filtered tap water in a crappy plastic bottle.

After carefully perusing the Fogey Fare I decided to throw caution to the wind and go for the Country Fried Steak. Since my wife was with me and at least part of The Stare was there, I skipped the bacon and opted for a side of green beans.

Waiting for the meal, I found myself feeling a little bit giddy, secure in the knowledge that I was saving both calories and cash, while everyone else in the restaurant would be none the wiser. They could go on assuming that I was, like Richard Gere, just prematurely gray.

Then the waiter brought our dinners. He strode up to our table with his firm waiter stride, carrying two steaming plates of food in his waiter hands, and asked in his booming waiter voice, "Who ordered the SENIOR CFS?"

Of course, I failed to dodge the obvious bullet. "I'm sorry," I said, "What is a cfs?"

"AH," he shrieked, deciding that my lack of understanding had to be due to a faulty hearing aid. "IT'S A SENIOR COUNTRY FRIED STEAK! SENIOR CFS! IT'S RIGHT WHERE YOU FOUND IT, ON THE SENIOR MENU! SENIOR CFS IS SENIOR COUNTRY FRIED STEAK! HA, HA! SENIOR!"

And so my cover was blown. As I ate my meal, my wife seemed completely oblivious to the snickers and stares from everyone else in Denny's that night. I swear I could hear them saying things like, "I understand all the stuff on the SENIOR MENU is a lot easier to chew..."

The final blow came when a gray-haired man with a long gray beard hobbled up to our table leaning on a walker with bright yellow tennis balls on the ends of the legs. He stopped, turned on his hearing aid, adjusted the air flow from his oxygen bottle, and said, "How was that meal, old timer? In just a few more years, I'll be able to order Grandpa Grub myself."

I kicked the walker out from under him and beat him senseless with his doggie bag.

Winter Olympics, NASCAR, and Red Wings; the Perfect Valentine's Day

This weekend my wife and I are enjoying a Perfect Storm of Really Cool Stuff.

On Friday the 2010 Winter Olympics* kicked off in Vancouver, British Columbia. There was a terrific Opening Ceremony highlighted by some teams marching in with hundreds of happy skiers and skaters waving at the crowd, while other teams were made up of a single athlete carrying a flag and followed by fifteen old bald government guys.

Canada, the host country, has been sounding uncharacteristically pugnacious about the competition this time around, but I'm pretty sure I saw the always fastidious and polite Canadian Curling

Team using their brooms on the way into the stadium to tidy up a bit.

On Monday we will celebrate President's Day, a time when all Americans set aside a few hours to reflect on the accomplishments of some of our nation's most revered leaders, and to buy mattresses.

Sandwiched in between, on Saturday, my friend scored us front-row tickets to take our wives to see the Detroit Red Wings. This was the last game before the NHL players take off to Vancouver, where they will split up into their national teams and spend a couple of weeks knocking each other's teeth out in Olympic competition.

The neatest moment of the evening came when my son sent my cell phone a picture from his cell phone of the TV screen where he was watching the game. It clearly showed my wife, my friend, his wife, and me standing up in our seats directly behind the visitor's bench. The others were cheering whatever was happening on the ice, and I was totally engrossed in sending my son a text message about how cool it was that I could just about read the coach's clipboard.

Today promises to be a really fun-packed day. For one thing, this is the Chinese New Year, the biggest holiday of all for Chinese people, tigers (we're kicking off the Year of the Tiger) and firecracker salesmen.

Today also marks the official start of the new NASCAR season with the Daytona 500, featuring those amazing driver interviews along the lines of, "Well, that there Number 82 Ex-Lax Toyota was runnin' real good for us today, until we got us a recall notice right after the last restart, on account of the rear axle broke and all the cup holders blowed up."

Oh yeah - and it's also Valentine's Day.

Valentine's Day is named after Saint Valentine, a Christian priest who lived (briefly) in third century Rome. According to the legend, when Emperor Claudius II was unsuccessful at beating Valentine to death with a club, he had him beheaded in the temple of Hallmark, the pagan God of Greeting Cards and Really Expensive Trinkets.

Eleven hundred years later, Geoffrey Chaucer, often referred to as the "Father of English Literature 101," apparently got wind of this deeply romantic story. Inspired, he penned a limerick for his wife, picked up a Whittemanne's Samplerre and some pansies on his way home from catching the afternoon beheadings at The Tower of London, and Valentine's Day as we know it was born.

Now every man who has been married for more than a couple of years knows that his short-term connubial happiness depends on coming up with something more interesting for his lady on

February 14 than a heart-shaped box of glop-filled chocolates. Unfortunately, most of us struggle with the idea that the gals never really respond all that well to practical stuff, like a gift set of little sandpaper pads they can use to grind the hair off their legs - even though the lady in the ad says that those things are the "most popular personal grooming product in Europe."

This Valentine's Day I am the luckiest man on the planet. My wife is a fanatic Red Wings fan, so the game last night scored big points, despite the fact that I can't take credit for anything beyond having the coolest friend ever and wearing a sweater that was easy to spot on television. She also loves NASCAR so much that it was her idea to go to a Winston Cup race at Michigan International Speedway on the first day of our honeymoon. And she is nearly as much of an Olympics junkie as I am. She will even watch live coverage of the Biathlon with me - for a while.

So all I've really needed to be a hero around our house this weekend has been a Valentine card and my natural mastery of the television DVR remote control. Maybe tomorrow I'll go for husbandly immortality and hit the mattress sales.

*The joy of the Olympic Games has been sadly overshadowed by the tragic training death of a young luge competitor from Georgia, Nodar Kumaritashvili.

The one consolation I can find is that this young man achieved a goal in his short life that only a select few people in all the world have achieved - he was an Olympian. Our thoughts and prayers are with his family, friends and fellow athletes.

Olympics Update - Ice Dancing Medals and Plenty of Spandex

Tonight I caught the finals in Olympic Ice Dancing. This sport has been evolving greatly over the past twenty years, to the point where these days there are a lot more creative costumes and routines and a lot fewer guys in greasy ponytails. I always make sure to watch for the quality of "the side-by-side twizzles."

The announcer told me to.

Two of the Ice Dance pairs are University of Michigan students. Meryl Davis and Charlie White went into the free dance with a good chance of winning a gold medal. Charlie recently said that about the only thing that could top a Michigan football game would be winning a medal at the Olympics.

The other couple, Emily Samuelson and Evan Bates (Evan is also a native Ann Arborite) never had a realistic shot at a top three finish, but they looked great and turned in a personal best. It kind of makes you wonder if the U of M should consider establishing a Department of Feathers and Sequins.

To make it more interesting, the Canadian team of Tessa Virtue and Scott Moir actually live here in Southeastern Michigan and train with Davis and White at the Arctic Edge Ice Arena in Canton. While all this local connection is very cool, that is not really what kept me glued to the screen. And it's not that I am not a particularly big fan of ice dancing; I have never watched so much as a single twizzle that did not get twizzed on Olympic ice.

No, just as long as the five rings are involved I will be willing to sit, transfixed, and cheer at the television through seven hours of pairs snow shoveling. And in the end, even if the winners are Plntzk and Smrtz Gmrnzkck of Kzlykyszstan, when they stand, shovels in hand, to get their gold medals and the Kzlykyszstan national anthem is played, I will get a little bit choked up, knowing that I just watched the Gmrnzkck brothers write a whole new page in the history of competitive slush chucking.

So I find myself following some pretty strange Olympic sports. We have "Freestyle Aerials," in which skiers rocket up a ramp that throws them fifty feet in the air, flip around furiously for about three seconds, then try to land in the snow with as few shattered bones and dislocated joints as possible.

Then there is "Snowboard Cross" and, for the first time in the Winter Olympics, "Ski Cross." These are exciting events which basically add up to racing down the hill while you participate in a high speed fist fight.

I also watch the less extreme sports like Ski Jumping (skinny Europeans in spandex with huge jump skis), Cross-country Skiing (skinny Europeans in spandex with skinny cross-country skis, cruising through the woods and eating granola bars), Curling (Canadians in golf shirts with brooms), and Biathlon (skinny Europeans in spandex with skinny cross-country skis, cruising through the woods with guns).

Then there are the speed skating events (enormous thighs and spandex-o-rama - they even wear spandex hoods!) and "sliding" events like Luge, Skeleton and Bobsled (trust me on this, there are quite a few bobsledders who would be a lot better off wearing almost anything other than spandex).

The payoff at the end of this particular evening of obsessive spectating was that Davis and

White wound up with a well-deserved Olympic silver medal. Virtue and Moir, those Canadians from Canton, MI won the gold.

And I got a little bit choked up when they played "O Canada" for a couple of kids who were having the best night of their hard-working young lives.

The Night the Lights Went Out

"Wow, some storm out there," says Dad, standing by the window and staring at the dark night sky.

Little Suzie looks up from her pink My Little Pony laptop computer "The National Weather Service data shows a strong occluded front moving in, and it's generating a major thermal inversion."

"Nya nya nya inversion," chants Todd Jr., aiming a kick at his younger sister's computer and narrowly missing as she pulls it out of harm's way. "It's more like the wind is going to blow the whole world into outer space."

"Yeah, Todd, that's exactly what it's like," says Little Suzie.

"It's a perfect night to stay inside and watch *American Idol*," says Mom.

At that moment the lights go out.

"Ahhhhhgh," says Mom.

"So much for *Idol*," says Little Suzie.

"Cool, we're in outer space," says Todd Jr.

"All right, nobody panic! I'll go get the flash light," says Dad, stepping on Bernie the Schnauzer.

"Yorrrrrrrrp!" says Bernie the Schnauzer.

Half an hour later the family is sitting on the living room floor huddled around the yellow pool of light from a birthday candle. "You know, I asked you to pick up some batteries for the flash-light," says Dad.

"When, exactly, did you ask me to do that?" asks Mom.

"I think you were pregnant with Todd Jr."

"So it's my fault that your flashlight batteries have been dead for nine years?"

"And it wouldn't kill you to have some real candles around the house."

"Happy birthday to me, happy birthday to me..." sings Todd Jr. as he blows out the candle.

As the room goes black, they all see a faint blue-white glow from the corner of the room, where Little Suzie sits in the arm chair with a small battery-operated book light clipped to the cover of Jane Austin's *Pride and Prejudice*.

"Hey, where did you get that?" shouts Todd Jr.

"Grandma got them for all of us last Christmas, remember?"

"Is that what that thing was for?" says Mom. "I thought it was to hold recipe cards."

"I've been using mine as a tie clip," says Dad.

"I couldn't find mine after I threw it at my stupid sister," says Todd Jr.

"I know," says Little Suzie, pulling a second book light from one of the pockets in her Barbie's Polar Expedition backpack.

"Say, that gives me an idea," says Dad.

Thirty minutes later Mom, Dad and Todd Jr. all have book lights duct taped to their foreheads. "Now we're just like coal miners," says Dad, "without the shovels and dynamite."

"And we probably have less risk of getting Black Lung disease here in the living room," says Little Suzie, who has managed to keep her book light on her book.

"Did you have to wrap the duct tape around my hair?" asks Mom.

"I'm Cyclops, the X-man," says Todd Jr., sprinting across the room, stepping on Bernie the Schnauzer, then slamming into the book case.

"Yorrrrrrrrp!" says Bernie. When the lights go back on a few hours later, Mom is asleep with People magazine in her lap. Dad has Bernie the

Schnauzer at his feet and both are snoring. Little Suzie has just learned that Darcy loved Elizabeth all along and wants to marry her. Todd Junior is still unconscious next to the book case.

And *Idol* is still unwatched.

Siri and Me

I finally got an iPhone. Mind you, I didn't get the trendy new iPhone 5 - the only model I could afford without hitting the lottery was a creaky old iPhone 4s. This means I will have to make do with a severely antiquated phone that lost its status as the most advanced technology in the world nearly three weeks ago.

I was forced to replace my old smartphone, Kierkegaard, because his battery died, and it was going to cost me more to replace the battery than to get the new phone. Besides, Kierkegaard kept pushing me over my data plan by sending me an endless stream of text messages going on and on about stuff like "...truth as subjectivity," or "...the fluidity of social identities" - sometimes in Danish. I figured it was time to move on, before I snapped and went all Hegelian on him.

My new iPhone is pretty nice. No, let me be slightly more precise - this thing is the greatest material addition to my life since the day I discovered beer and barbecued ribs.

My new iPhone's name is Siri, and Siri is my new best friend. She can look at my itinerary, have a little chat with the weather satellite, then tell me whether I need to take a raincoat on my trip. If I need to reschedule a meeting, she can update my calendar and send a lame-but-basically-plausible excuse to the Siris of all the other people involved. If I need to know who it was that caught the Katy, and what exactly she left behind for me to ride, in a matter of seconds Siri can remind me that it was "My Baby" and "A Mule" (in that order).

I am aware that a lot of people might read this and say, "What's the big deal? Almost everybody has an iPhone these days. Our dog groomer has one. In fact, the groomer just picked one up for his schnauzer."

It is true that the iPhone's claim to exclusivity has faded a bit. My thoughts fondly wander back to the golden days when only the coolest and most affluent people could own an iPhone. You could recognize these people by the smug look on their faces, the snow white ear buds in their ears, and the cheap second phones they all carried so they could actually make and receive phone calls.

So far, my life with Siri has been a nonstop whirlwind of discovery. When you push the round button below the screen, dozens of cool looking little square pictures appear. When I tap on one of these square things, stuff happens. Sometimes I get my email. Sometimes I get a doppler radar map of the weather in the area around Springer, New Mexico. Sometimes I get to watch a twenty-two minute YouTube video of some young guy in a wife beater t-shirt and boxer shorts, sitting in a Barcalounger with a Siamese cat in his lap and eating Froot Loops.

The email, weather map, and Froot Loop Film are what is known in the smartphone biz as "apps." I discovered these back when I first got Kierkegaard, and I decided back then that "app" must be short for something like "app-arently you have a lot of time on your hands to download this kind of crap."

Most of the "Featured Apps" you can get are games involving rocket powered lasers and zombies. My favorite app, though, is called "Apple Maps." This is a cool little program that figures out exactly where you are and then shows you on a map. If you take your fingers and kind of pinch across the screen, you can instantly find out what continent you're on.

If you want to learn how to get somewhere, you can just ask Siri. She'll launch Apple Maps, pinpoint where you are and where your destination is, then plot a route to get there. Then she'll kind of bug you to get moving; "Go north one quarter mile and turn right. I said, 'go north.' One quarter mile north and turn right. Get going. Seriously. Look, if you're not going to go north, why the hell did you ask me in the first place?"

Now, I've heard some iPhone users gripe about the accuracy of Apple Maps. Okay, I admit that Siri's routes can occasionally take you from Detroit to Indianapolis by way of Bangladesh. But to all those complainers I say, "Where's your sense of adventure? Bangladesh is beautiful this time of year."

At least, that's what Siri says.

Fighting the Resolutionary War

It's New Years! Time to write up your List!

We all know pretty much how this resolution thing works. You approach the coming year with good intentions, so you write down a bunch of stuff like, "I hereby resolve to tighten the screw in the downstairs door frame."

As your List grows, so does its variety; you want to lose 30 pounds, write a historical novel about the turbulent days of The Captain and Tennille Show, and maybe find out exactly what is in that drawer in the kitchen - the one over by the window that's got something jammed in it so that you haven't been able to get it open since 1997.

By the time the ball falls on New Year's Eve, you have your List stuck on the refrigerator under the Little Bear with Skis and a Santa Hat refrigerator magnet, ready to fuel your all-out assault on all those personal priorities. OK, maybe it did take you longer to write down most of the tasks on your list than it would have taken you to do them, but still...

On New Year's day you look at your List with satisfaction, and briefly consider tackling something on it. But hey, you think, you've got a whole year to get this stuff done, and there's some eggnog and half a bottle of Wild Turkey left from last night, so...

Sometime in early February you open the 'fridge to see if there is any milk in there that is not totally solid, and you notice the List. Meh, it's not even spring yet...

In April you catch a glimpse of the List as you search frantically for some form you need for your income taxes, the one the accountant asked you for back in January. You briefly consider working on that kitchen drawer, since it would be a lot more interesting than the tax form, then you spot the package of Chips Ahoy next to the microwave...

In early July you go to grab a beer and knock the Little Bear with Skis and a Santa Hat refrigerator magnet off the 'fridge, and the List falls into the dog's water dish. Eventually the dog gets thirsty, so you fish out the list and set it by the window to dry in the sun...

By mid-August the List has fairly well dried out, but there is an expired Subway coupon under the Little Bear With Skis and a Santa hat refrigerator magnet, so you throw away the aged-to-unreadable receipt under the Kitty Cat With a Fish in its Mouth refrigerator magnet and post the list up high on the freezer door. The screw in that door isn't tightening itself, you know...

It's September, and you have just finished chipping the bottle of petrified milk out of the refrigerator, when you notice the List and decide to get cracking on that historical novel. After ten minutes of research you discover that The Captain And Tennille Show ran for less than a season, and nobody actually watched it, so you decide to instead do your novel about the childhood of Millard Fillmore. You edit the List accordingly...

In early November your son drops by for a visit and yanks open the kitchen drawer by the window, shattering the plastic ruler that's been holding it shut, and revealing fifteen dead "C" cell batteries, several tubes of dried-up Super Glue, a combination padlock for which nobody knows the combination, a toy claw hammer from the dollar store, a cat's eye marble, some sort of putty that has melted then solidified around a bunch of loose thumb tacks, a rusty box cutter, six rolls of

Scotch tape, and an extension cord. You shut the drawer by the window, causing the toy hammer to shift so that the handle pops up and jams the drawer again, then you go to the refrigerator and cross the first item off your List...

On Christmas day, as you are putting a platter of leftover ham in the 'fridge, you notice the List, dog-eared and yellowed, just about to slip out from under the Kitty Cat With a Fish in its Mouth refrigerator magnet. You decide to go ahead and tighten that screw in the door, thereby checking another item off the list. If you can just find a screwdriver. Woah, there's some eggnog and Wild Turkey left...

And then it's New Years Eve. As you get some ice out of the refrigerator to make Mojitos, the List slides out from under the Kitty Cat With a Fish in its Mouth refrigerator magnet and flutters to the floor, sliding well back under the refrigerator and out of reach. You smile to yourself and grab a pen to write up a new list. Item one, you always wanted to write a light comedy about Attila the Hun...

Happy New Year, Everybody!

Down to the Sea in a Pontoon Boat

Part I - In Which We Find the Perfect Boat

There are some people who say that Pontoon Boats are just for deaf old men in Sans a Belt slacks. To that I say, "What? Speak up!"

One of the fondest memories I have of my first year living here on the lake was one fine day toward the end of the summer when I stood next to my neighbor Harold, gazing at a couple of youngsters being pulled on a rubber tube behind a speedboat. As we watched the kids being pounded to mush and enjoyed their blood-curdling shrieks of terror, Harold turned to me and said, "You know, we ought to go in together and buy a used pontoon boat."

I nodded, squinted at the sun glinting off the lifeless body of a child who had been hurled off

the tube, grabbed hold of the polyester Sans a Belt
slacks that at that moment had materialized on
me, hitched them up tight under my armpits, and
said, "You know, that sounds like a great idea!"

And so on that momentous afternoon nearly
twenty years ago began the great adventure
of the lake-going vessel now generally known
around these parts as the "HMS," or "Harold &
Mike's Scow."

Now back in those days, pretty much all I
knew about pontoon boats was that they had
pontoons. Also, people who had them seemed to
enjoy packing a very large number of other people
and coolers full of beer onto them, which I found
interesting. Harold gently told me that there was
a little bit more to consider in buying a pontoon
boat, and suggested that we let him do the research involved in finding us a boat. I was fine
with that, so I pretty much forgot about the whole
thing for a few weeks.

Then one evening, as I sat on the shore thinking about how much I hated Sans a Belt slacks
and wondering how I could be wearing socks
with sandals when I didn't actually own any
socks, Harold came over and said, "I've found
the perfect boat for us!" He explained to me that
it was about twelve years old, was a little bit sun
faded, the top was worn out, and there was a little

bit of crud on the pontoons that would "... chip right off." On the upside, it had nice big pontoons, the most reliable engine known to man, and the price was right.

I told him that the boat sounded like my idea of heaven.

A few days later we hitched a borrowed "pontoon trailer" to my little truck and drove to a lake 38.7 miles away to pick up our treasure.

The first adventure we faced involved the pontoon trailer itself. If you've never seen one of these things, they look like they are made from a gigantic erector set, a huge lattice of pipes on wheels. They are also really long, so that when you drive around a corner and forget you have it trolling along back there, you kind of accumulate stuff around the fenders, like stop signs and school crossing guards.

The plot thickened considerably when we got to the lake, picked the stop signs and crossing guards out of the fenders, and realized that neither Harold nor I had any idea whatsoever how to put a pontoon boat on a pontoon boat trailer. The thing had a baffling spider web of cables and pulleys, from which Harold was able to get me disentangled in just under an hour, with a minimal loss of blood.

We eventually discovered that if you uncoupled something Harold identified as the "flippy doo" and cranked "that thingerwhappy over there," the frame-amajig would come up and raise the boat off the ground. A little bit.

Unfortunately, raising the boat off the ground a "little bit" left the pontoons just a few inches above the pavement (we found out, years later, that if we had only known enough to attach the loopiebob to the hookerdoodle, we would have been able to crank it really high, raising the center of gravity enough that the boat could then have toppled off the trailer and into the first busy intersection we went through).

I was a tad more optimistic about the whole driving with low ground clearance thing than Harold was, since the "little bit of crud" I had already volunteered to clean off the pontoons turned out to be a caked-on coating of lime more than an inch thick, and I figured that with a little luck we might scrape some of it off on the way home.

It took us more than four hours to drive the 38.7 miles back home, since we couldn't go more than about 11 miles per hour. And we actually did manage to shave the pontoons down a bit; we found that railroad tracks were especially effective for this.

We eventually managed to get our treasure home and tucked away in a covered warehouse, where we could spend the next eight months making it ship-shape and ready to launch the following spring.

Next up, Part II - Spending Eight Months Chipping Crud Off the Perfect Boat.

Down to the Sea in a Pontoon Boat
Part II - In Which I Chip Crud Off the Perfect Boat

In our last installment, my neighbor Harold and I decided to buy a pontoon boat together. If you've never seen a pontoon boat, what we're talking about is basically a motorized patio floating on a couple of giant aluminum cans. We had come to the conclusion that a pontoon boat might serve as the ideal platform for, among other things, the sun-drenched and leisurely consumption of alcohol.

Our story left off just after we brought our "new" boat home using a trailer we didn't entirely know how to use, resulting in two pontoon-esque furrows all along the 38.7 miles of back roads between here and Grass Lake, MI. It was October, so instead of popping the boat right into the lake we went ahead and put it in "Dry Dock" - four cinder blocks in a big garage.

Harold was an expert woodworker, so he tucked right into making new solid oak table tops, complete with recessed drink holders, for every horizontal surface on the boat. He also knew how to fine-tune the engine, grease the lower unit, beef up the wiring, patch the carpeting, touch up the paint, and repair the stereo system.

I was able put my deep reservoir of knowledge and experience to good use as well; I slid under the boat with a paint scraper and spent the winter hacking away at the thick coat of lime and dried algae on the pontoons.

This turned out to be a pretty effective division of labor. Once Harold got the stereo working, I could crank it up and lie on my back under the boat, hacking away in time with Led Zeppelin's "Dazed and Confused" (my personal theme song). As the weeks and months went by I became a connoisseur of the sort of background music best suited for crud-chiseling. I found that groups like AC/DC or Nine Inch Nails were too rowdy for whacking away at soft aluminum pontoons, while songs by Barry Manilow or The Eagles would generally take me anywhere from nausea to coma.

In about the middle of March, I made a few calls and ended up trading some hockey equipment and a bag of cash to an upholsterer in return for a new "Bimini Top" and "Playpen Cover." Neither of these things is nearly as interesting (or sexy) as the names imply. A Playpen Cover is actually a huge canvas canopy that snaps over the railings to keep the sun from cooking the furniture. A Bimini is a sort of convertible top that opens up to keep the sun from cooking the boaters and the beer.

As the winter wore on and my pile of crud scrapings began to pose an avalanche hazard, it felt like Harold and I were making real progress. Finally one day in May, Harold announced that it was time for us to schedule the Scow's christening and launch.

The trailer we had borrowed to pick up the boat was no longer available, so we decided to find a company we could hire to transport our nautical treasure from the garage to the lake. After a lot of discussion, we decided to go with someone who actually knew how to use a pontoon boat trailer. And maybe take a few notes.

A couple of days before SL (Scow Launch) Day, Harold charged up the battery and put the finishing touches on the interior. On the last night in Dry Dock I whiled away the final hours chipping crud in time with "Stairway To Heaven," along with a little upbeat Aerosmith ("Dude

Looks Like A Lady") to get me through the last nasty bits.

On the morning of SL Day I tried to act like a seasoned boat-launcher guy. The previous week I had bought a new Sea Doo (which, if you've never seen one, is basically a floating crotch rocket) and I was looking for any excuse to use the new toy. So, in what we writers call "ominous foreshadowing," I gave Harold my best boat-launcher guy smile and said, "Why don't you go ahead and throw the boat in the water, while I hop on the Sea Doo and meet you over at the launch."

Next up, Part III - In Which the Perfect Boat Doesn't Actually Sink.

Down to the Sea
in a Pontoon Boat
Part III - In Which the Perfect Boat Doesn't Actually Sink

When we last left our heroes, Harold and Mike, they were about to launch their newly re-stored pontoon boat, which we've come to know as "Harold & Mike's Scow." As we pick up the action, Harold is riding to the DNR site with the truck pulling the boat trailer, while Mike is setting off to meet him astride his trusty Sea Doo...

Even though it was a nice warm day in May, the water in the lake was still pretty cold, so I stopped at the house to put on a wet suit. Then I uncovered and dry-fired the Sea Doo, cranked it down off the hoist, checked the oil, hopped on, started the engine, and idled halfway across the lake to warm it up.

In other words, it took me quite a while to get moving. So long, in fact, that I was surprised that I didn't run into Harold and the Scow coming the other way.

The reason for this became clear when I cruised into the cove near the launch and found Harold sitting aboard the Scow, gazing at the puffy clouds in the sky and looking relaxed, drifting silently toward the middle of the lake. I came alongside, killed the engine on the Sea Doo, and said, "What's up?"

"Nothing much," he said. "Say, just out of curiosity, were you doing some last-minute work on the pontoons last night?"

"Yes." I nodded humbly, basking in the glow of a job well done. "I chopped away at those suckers until nearly midnight."

"I was just sitting here and thinking how nice they looked."

"Thank you."

"You're welcome. And, also out of curiosity, did you happen to have the stereo on while you were working?"

"Yes. And let me just say that those speakers you wired up sound fantastic."

"Thank you. They do sound pretty good."

"They made the job a lot easier."

"I'll bet they did. So anyway, is there is any possibility that when you were finished, you just might have left the stereo running?"

"Oh." My pride descended to half-bask. "So, the engine wouldn't fire up?"

"Not so much as a spark."

"Dead battery?"

"That would be my guess."

"The battery you charged up yesterday?"

"Yep."

"The one that was in great shape yesterday afternoon when we tested the engine?"

"Yep, that one."

"Oh. Sorry."

"Don't mention it. It's actually been pretty pleasant sitting out here on the lake. Peaceful."

"Since you don't have to put up with the sound of an engine running?"

"Exactly."

We decided that we had enjoyed about enough peace, so we grabbed a rope that Harold had the foresight to have on board and hooked our twenty-four foot pontoon boat up to the five foot Sea Doo. Then we headed for our home port, with Harold looking as dignified as possible riding a pontoon boat being towed by a jet ski.

Now, if there is one thing you can count on after many years of marriage it is the unconditional support of your loving spouse in times of hardship and tribulation. She will stand at your side, strong and unflinching, even though the rest of the world heaps scorn on you.

OK, anyone who has actually been married knows better than that load of crap.

Harold's wife Donna had apparently spotted us coming and notified my wife. They stood on the sea wall, doubled over in laughter and taking pictures for my wife to post in her carefully-maintained Scrapbook of Stupid Stuff Mike Has Done.

Over the nineteen years since that day, that old boat has witnessed some serious fun and the consumption of a fair number of beers. Harold went on to the Next Big Adventure a few years ago, my friend Tom has taken his place as the other half of the Scow's essential crew, and the party keeps cruising on. But every now and then we stop and take a minute to dump a little beer on the deck in Harold's honor.

After all, the whole thing was his idea.

About The Author

Mike Ball is an award-winning humorist and author of *What I've Learned... So Far,* who lives and writes on the shores of Whitmore Lake, Michigan, sharing a roof with his wife Nancy and a psychotic Siamese cat. Their home is just North of Ann Arbor, home of the University of Michigan and one of the world's most fertile breeding grounds for hippies, folk singers, and Budweiser-soaked football fans.

In addition to cranking out his weekly humor column, Mike is a musician and the founder of Lost Voices, a Michigan non-profit group that designs and implements therapeutic roots music writing and performing programs for incarcerated and at-risk youth. As the front man of the band Dr. Mike & The Sea Monkeys, he brings his columns to musical life with such crowd pleasers as "Carlson the Pissed Off Angel," "At Least I've Got Most of My Hair," and "The Colonscopy Song."

Mike has spent most of his adult life writing and producing columns, ads, brochures, slogans, songs, menus, and anything else that needed writing, including a eulogy for a dog. During the Internet Boom of the 1990s he wrote a monthly column for a national information technology-oriented human resources magazine (now there's a combination that just screams humor!) called Itrecruitermag. These pieces covered such topics as "What to Do When You Run Into Your Boss at the Career Fair" and "So, You've Been Downsized. Sucks to Be You."

In 2003 Mike won the Erma Bombeck Award, and he was a finalist for the 2011 Robert Benchley Award. *What I've Learned So Far...* is syndicated and has online readers in eleven countries (that we know of).

Mike also spent some time as a competitive pairs water skier. He and various partners won numerous awards, including the 1997 Florida State Show Ski Championship at Cypress Gardens, the 2000 Indoor World Championship, the 2002 Michigan State Expert Division Championship, and the 2002 Division II National Championship. The better-looking member of the pair shown here is the amazing Megan Atkins.

Connect with Mike Ball Online
http://learnedsofar.com
Twitter: @tagmike
Facebook.com/MikeBallAuthor

Also by Mike Ball:

What I've Learned... So Far Part I
Bikes, Docks & Slush Nuggets

and

What I've Learned... So Far Part II
Angels, Chimps, & Tater Mitts

20202064R00195

Made in the USA
Middletown, DE
19 May 2015